STERLING
Test Prep

LAW ESSENTIALS

Torts

Governing Law

3rd edition

3   2   1

ISBN-13: 978-1-9547251-0-2

Sterling Test Prep products are available at quantity discounts.

For more information, contact info@sterling–prep.com.

Sterling Test Prep
6 Liberty Square #11
Boston, MA 02109

©2022 Sterling Test Prep
Published by Sterling Test Prep
Printed in the U.S.A.

Customer Satisfaction Guarantee

Your feedback is important because we strive to provide the highest quality prep materials. Email us comments or suggestions.

info@sterling–prep.com

We reply to emails – check your spam folder

Thank you for choosing our book!

STERLING
Test Prep

Thousands of students use our study aids to prepare for law school exams and to pass the bar!

Passing the bar is essential for admission to practice law and launching your legal career.

This preparation guide describes the principles of substantive law governing the correct answers to exam questions. It was developed by legal professionals and law instructors who possess extensive credentials and have been admitted to practice law in several jurisdictions. The content is clearly presented and systematically organized for targeted preparation.

The performance on individual questions has been correlated with success or failure on the bar. By analyzing previously administered exams, the authors identified these predictive items and assembled the rules of law that govern the answers to questions tested. Learn the essential governing law to make fine-line distinctions among related principles and decide between tough choices on the exam. This knowledge is vital to excel in law school finals and pass the bar exam.

We look forward to being an essential part of your preparation and wish you great success in the legal profession!

210630vgr

Law Essentials series

Constitutional Law	Criminal Law and Criminal Procedure
Contracts	Business Associations
Evidence	Conflict of Laws
Real Property	Family Law
Torts	Secured Transactions
Civil Procedure	Trusts and Estates

Visit our Amazon store

Comprehensive Glossary of Legal Terms

Over 2,100 essential legal terms defined and explained. An excellent reference source for law students, practitioners and readers seeking an understanding of legal vocabulary and its application.

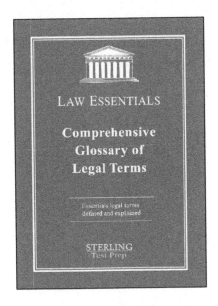

Landmark U.S. Supreme Court Cases: Essential Summaries

Learn important constitutional cases that shaped American law. Understand how the evolving needs of society intersect with the U.S. Constitution. Short summaries of seminal Supreme Court cases focused on issues and holdings.

Visit our Amazon store

Table of Contents

TORTS GOVERNING LAW *(continued)*

TORTS GOVERNING LAW (*continued*)

EXAM INFORMATION, PREP & TEST-TAKING STRATEGIES (*continued*)

EXAM INFORMATION, PREP & TEST-TAKING STRATEGIES (*continued*)

Essay Preparation Strategies and Essay-Writing Suggestions (*continued*)

APPENDIX (*continued*)

APPENDIX (*continued*)

Torts Governing Law

Torts topics tested on the exam are predictable. Master the principles to excel on Torts questions. The most frequently tested Torts issues are negligence (including duties of children), intentional torts, strict liability, products liability, premises liability, vicarious liability (may be coupled with Agency on the MEE). On the MEE, Torts is tested about every other cycle and generally is not combined with other subjects. However, it may be combined with Business Associations (e.g., Agency and vicarious liability).

The statements herein were compiled by analyzing released Torts questions and setting forth the principles of law governing the correct answers. Review these principles before preparing answers to practice Torts questions. Memorize this governing law and understand how it applies to the correct answer.

Per the National Conference of Bar Examiners (NCBE), assume that survival actions and wrongful death claims are available. Joint and several liability, with pure comparative negligence, is the relevant rule unless otherwise indicated.

STERLING
Test Prep

Tort Law – Overview

Definitions

Tort – a non-contractual civil wrong.

Tortfeasor – one who commits a tort.

Personal injury – lawsuits for money damages for injuries; the most common personal injury cases involve automobile accidents.

Cause of action – the basis upon which a lawsuit may be filed in court.

Workers' compensation applies to those injured in the course of employment.

Punitive damage – money awards meant to punish and discourage such behavior.

Intentional torts

An intentional tort is one in which the party committing the tort intends to do the *act* (*knowing* – or with a substantial certainty that – it will cause an injury).

In situations where the same act is a tort and crime, the cases will be handled separately (civil and criminal court proceedings) within the legal system.

Intentional torts against persons

Assault – apprehension of imminent harm

Battery – unlawful contact with another

False imprisonment

Defamation of character

Misappropriation of the right to publicity

Invasion of the right to privacy

Intentional infliction of emotional distress

Intentional torts against property

Trespass to land

Trespass to and conversion of personal property

Unintentional torts (negligence)

Elements of Negligence

1) *Duty* – defendant owed a duty of care to the plaintiff.

2) *Breach* – defendant breached the duty of care.

3) *Causation* – defendant's negligent act caused the plaintiff's injury.

4) *Damages* – plaintiff suffered an injury.

Special Negligence Doctrine

Negligent infliction of emotional distress

Negligence *per se* (i.e., violates a statute or regulation)

res ipsa loquitur (Latin, *the thing speaks for itself*)

Strict (absolute) liability – liability without fault

Defective products (e.g., product liability)

Ultra-hazardous activities (e.g., blasting activities)

Dangerous animals (e.g., wild animals)

Intentional Torts

Children under the age of 7, while not liable for negligence as a matter of law, can be liable for intentional torts if they possess the requisite intent.

Assault

To render a defendant liable for assault, the plaintiff must prove that the:

1) defendant intended at the time of the act to commit a harmful or offensive bodily contact or instill apprehension of such contact, and

2) plaintiff was placed in apprehension of such imminent bodily harm.

No actual damages must be proven to complete the tort of assault.

Intent to cause apprehension of the offensive bodily contact is the state of mind required for assault.

Intent to make actual contact is not required.

The apprehension must be that the contact will be immediate.

A conditional threat of harm in the future does not constitute an assault but could constitute intentional infliction of emotional distress.

The tort of assault cannot be accomplished by words that create the required apprehension unless there is an actual or apparent ability to cause offensive contact.

Where the defendant intends to commit an assault, but not a battery, and the conduct causing the assault results in a battery, the intent to commit the assault fulfills the battery's intent requirement.

There is a privilege to commit an assault in self-defense, defense of others, and to eject trespassers.

These privileges exist if the actor reasonably believed that the circumstances called for the conduct necessary to use an assault in one of these privileged circumstances, even if the actor was mistaken.

Battery

There are four elements for the tort of battery:

1) there must be an intent to cause a touching,

2) there must be a touching,

3) there must not be "consent" to the touching, and

4) the touching must be harmful or offensive.

Proof of actual damages is not required.

The intent element

If the defendant lacks the mental capacity to know that they engaged in touching, they are not liable for battery.

If a party intended only to assault the plaintiff (placing in fear of imminent danger) and instead caused a touching, the intent to commit the assault is the intent necessary for the tort of battery.

Reckless or even willful conduct does not provide the mental intent for battery.

The consent element

Even if consent to physical contact is given during an athletic contest, an intentional force beyond the scope of that consent will result in an actionable battery.

The touching element

Ordinarily, the defendant commits battery by touching the actual person of the plaintiff.

The touching of an object close to the plaintiff, such as an item of clothing or a horse on which the plaintiff is riding, satisfies this element of the tort.

Placing in motion events that will cause an offensive contact constitutes the offensive contact necessary for a battery.

The defense of privilege

There is a privilege to use reasonable force to commit a battery in self-defense, defense of others, and eject trespassers.

These privileges exist if the actor reasonably believed they acted in the circumstances giving rise to the privilege and that the force was reasonable, even if there was a mistake.

An unreasonable belief will not sustain the privilege.

If a party is privileged to commit a battery on a third party, unintentional touching of the plaintiff will not give the plaintiff a cause of action in battery.

However, the plaintiff may have a cause of action in negligence.

An individual has the privilege to commit a battery if the battery prevents an actual injury to the plaintiff, and the actor reasonably believes that the plaintiff is in danger of receiving an actual injury.

False imprisonment

The tort of false imprisonment contains the following elements:

1) confinement (generally, knowledge by the confined)

2) intent to confine

3) lack of consent to the confinement

Since false imprisonment is an intentional tort, no actual damage must be proved as an element of the tort.

Confinement

Confinement occurs when the plaintiff's ability to move from their location is restricted.

Physical force to restrict that movement is unnecessary.

Confinement requires the plaintiff to be aware of the limitation on movement. If the plaintiff knows of a reasonable alternate route to avoid the limitation of movement, they are not confined.

Intent for false imprisonment

The defendant's intentional act must cause the plaintiff's confinement.

Privilege as a defense for false imprisonment

A shopkeeper has the privilege to use reasonable force to detain someone reasonably suspected of shoplifting for a limited time, only to determine if that person has engaged in shoplifting.

A citizen has the right to arrest, which constitutes confinement if they reasonably believe a felony has been committed and reasonably believe that the person detained was the felon.

A police officer has the right to arrest if executing an arrest warrant or arresting for a felony or misdemeanor committed in their presence.

Therefore, a person who has the right to arrest is privileged to confine and has a defense against a claim for false imprisonment.

A wrongful arrest constitutes false imprisonment.

The fact that the person arrested was not guilty of the crime for which they were arrested does not automatically give rise to a cause of action for false imprisonment.

Trespass to land

If the defendant intends to occupy the space they physically occupy, a mistaken belief that the land occupied is not the plaintiff's land will not be a defense to trespass.

Actual damages are not necessary for an action of trespass to land.

Nominal damages can be recovered.

If the defendant is unintentionally placed upon the plaintiff's land, there is no trespass.

However, there could be an action in negligence if the defendant is unintentionally placed upon the plaintiff's land. The negligence action requires damage to the plaintiff's land.

Nominal damages are not sufficient in a negligence action.

Whether express or implied, the consent of the landowner to the defendant's presence on the property is a defense to trespass.

A person may be privileged under emergency circumstances to enter upon another's property to protect the person or property.

An entry under such circumstances will not constitute a trespass.

The person using the property must pay the owner or possessor for damage done to the property.

A property owner has a right to use reasonable means to bar people from their land (through fences or obstructions) and has a privilege to use reasonable force to eject a trespasser but does not have the right to commit battery on the trespasser not connected with the ejection.

A landowner is not liable to a trespasser for ordinary negligence but is liable if they could have prevented the injury after becoming aware of it.

Conversion

Conversion requires *substantial interference* with the plaintiff's personal property.

If the defendant has wrongfully appropriated the plaintiff's personal property and substantially damaged or lost it, or if the defendant refuses to return it after demand, the plaintiff has an action in conversion for the full value of the property at the time when the defendant first appropriated it.

Trespass to chattels

The tort of trespass to chattels (i.e., personal property), unlike trespass to land, requires proof of damage or actual interference with the plaintiff's possessory rights to the personal property.

Trespass to chattels occurs when there is interference with chattels, which is not substantial enough to constitute conversion.

The damages recoverable for trespass to chattels are limited to the diminution in the chattels' value and compensation for the plaintiff's lost use of the chattels.

Intentional infliction of emotional distress

The tort of intentional infliction of emotional distress is composed of the following elements:

1) extreme and outrageous conduct by the defendant,

2) intent of the defendant to cause severe emotional distress.

The plaintiff must suffer emotional distress but need not suffer physical harm to collect damages for embarrassment and mental anguish.

The defendant's conduct must ordinarily be so extreme or outrageous that it would likely cause emotional distress in a person of ordinary sensibilities. However, conduct can be extreme or outrageous if the defendant knows of the plaintiff's unusual sensibilities and tailors conduct to cause the plaintiff's emotional distress.

The defendant who commits an intentional tort might be liable for intentional infliction of emotional distress to a family member of the victim if the defendant knew that a family member was a witness to that intentional tort.

Negligent infliction of emotional distress

If the defendant's negligence causes damage to an individual, a person who does not suffer physical injury as a direct result of the negligent conduct can recover for negligent infliction of emotional distress only if they:

> 1) experience some actual physical harm as opposed to embarrassment or mental anguish, from the defendant's negligence, and,
>
> 2) are within the zone of danger or,
>
> 3) witness harm to a family member.

The plaintiff could recover for negligent infliction of emotional distress only if the defendant's conduct were sufficient to cause emotional distress in a person of standard sensitivities.

Once this objective test is met, the plaintiff can recover for emotional harm suffered, even if the harm is unusual.

Negligent infliction of emotional distress caused by negligence in handling a loved one's remains is compensable without proof of physical harm.

If the plaintiff only suffers property damage, as opposed to a personal physical injury caused by the defendant's negligence, damages for emotional distress cannot be recovered.

Once a plaintiff suffers physical injury caused by the defendant's negligence, mental distress is an element of damages. The distinct elements of the tort of negligent infliction of emotional distress need not be met for the plaintiff to recover.

Nuisance

Private nuisance

Nuisance is a theory of tort liability independent of intentional torts and negligent torts.

A plaintiff has a cause of action in nuisance when the defendant's use of neighboring land unreasonably interferes with the use and enjoyment of their land.

If there is an actual physical invasion of the plaintiff's land by the defendant's use of neighboring land, the cause of action is for trespass rather than a nuisance.

Nuisance is applicable when there is detrimental use but not a physical invasion of the plaintiff's land.

A nuisance is a private nuisance if it unreasonably interferes with only a limited number of neighbors' use and enjoyment of their land.

Those neighbors have a cause of action for private nuisance.

Unreasonable interference

Land use before a neighbor arrives is a factor but not dispositive when considering if a use unreasonably interferes with the neighbor's land.

If the neighbor claiming unreasonable interference uses their land in a manner requiring freedom from regular neighborhood activity, they are unlikely to prevail in a suit with a landowner who has been conducting such regular activity before the plaintiff moved into the neighborhood.

The more objectionable the use of the defendant's land, the more likely that an adjoining landowner, even a newcomer, will prevail in nuisance.

The fact that a particular use is permitted on the offending land by local land-use regulations does not per se establish that the use is not a nuisance. However, it is evidence of the reasonableness of use.

Courts can impose injunctive or damage remedies in nuisance cases.

The social utility of land use, which affects neighboring land, such as an operation that recycles material, influences the court's choice of remedy, and may result in the denial of injunctive relief.

Public nuisance

A nuisance is a public nuisance if it interferes with the use and enjoyment of a large area of neighboring land.

In general, only public agencies have standing to pursue the public nuisance cause of action.

A private plaintiff has standing to sue for public nuisance if the harm affects the plaintiff's land more directly and intensely than it does to the larger area affected.

Strict Liability

Product liability for manufacturers

To prevail on a strict liability theory, a plaintiff must prove the product:

1) was defective when it left the defendant's hands,

2) was rendered unreasonably dangerous by that defect, and

3) caused the injury.

The defendant's exercise of utmost care in manufacturing or handling the product will not defeat the plaintiff's strict liability claim if the product was defective, dangerous, and caused an injury.

A product could be defective because it is unreasonably dangerous, even if the manufacturer did not know the danger and even if a regulatory authority approved its distribution.

The plaintiff must prove the defective product was causally related to the plaintiff's injuries.

Suits against users of a product that causes injury must be based upon negligence, not strict liability.

Defenses for manufacturers

If the product was not defective when it left the manufacturer's or vendor's possession, alteration of the product after it left their possession is a defense to the plaintiff's strict liability action.

Plaintiffs can sue on a strict liability theory for harm from unavoidably unsafe drugs (including blood) only if the supplier does not notify the physician of the dangers.

Assumption of the risk is a defense in strict product liability actions.

In jurisdictions that recognize comparative negligence for product liability, the defense of assumption of the risk merges into that defense.

In those jurisdictions, the plaintiff's damages can be reduced but not eliminated when they assumed the risk or is negligent.

The plaintiff's misuse would not be a complete defense unless that misuse were unforeseeable. However, it can be the basis of negligence in a comparative negligence jurisdiction to reduce damages.

The following are NOT defenses to a strict liability action:

1) Privity between the plaintiff and the manufacturer is not a condition that must be satisfied in a strict liability case against the manufacturer or seller of a product.

    Liability extends to foreseeable users and bystanders injured.

2) Negligence in using a product by the product owner, which harms a third party, is not a defense in product liability cases brought by the third party but might be the basis for contribution among joint tortfeasors.

3) Jurisdictions that retain contributory negligence as a defense in negligence do not recognize it as a defense in strict liability actions.

Failure to warn

Failure of the product's label to warn of dangers of a specific use can cause the product to be defective for product liability purposes when used in a way the manufacturer should have warned against, even though the product is not dangerous if used in other ways.

If the basis of product liability is a failure to warn about a dangerous product, the dangerous or defective nature of the product is not the relevant issue.

If the defect consisted of a failure to warn, the plaintiff must show that the injury would not have occurred if the warning had been made.

Product liability for subcontractors

An assembler of a dangerous product is liable on a product liability theory if the product's dangerous nature was caused by the defective parts supplied by a third party, included in the finished product.

If a product is dangerous because of a defect in a component, the finished part manufacturer and the defective component manufacturer are jointly liable in strict product liability.

The manufacturer of the component would be required to indemnify the finished product manufacturer if the finished-product manufacturer is required to pay the judgment.

Product liability for vendors

Strict liability in tort applies to a seller who is not the manufacturer when:

1) the seller is engaged in the business of selling the type of product involved,

2) the product is expected to and does reach the user without substantial change in condition in which it was sold, and

3) such a seller would have a claim for indemnification from the manufacturer if the manufacturer caused the defect.

Claims in negligence

Plaintiffs have the right to sue manufacturers and retailers for negligently manufacturing or selling products that cause harm.

In such suits, the defendant's evidence of due care in manufacturing the product or the retailer in inspecting the product is relevant.

In jurisdictions that retain contributory negligence, it is a defense in a product liability action based on negligence.

A manufacturer is not liable for negligence if it used reasonable care to inspect the parts assembled into a finished product.

Abnormally dangerous or ultra-hazardous activities

Ultra-hazardous activity is that which:

1) is not common in the area and

2) involves a risk of serious harm to others, which cannot be eliminated by the exercise of utmost care.

Blasting is an ultra-hazardous activity.

Defendants are liable in strict liability for abnormally dangerous operations.

A person hiring an independent contractor to engage in an ultra-hazardous activity is vicariously liable for torts.

A plaintiff can recover in strict liability for damage caused by the defendant permitting substances (commonly liquids) to escape from their land onto the neighbor's land.

If the person engaging in the ultra-hazardous activity warns of the danger, and the victim ignores the warnings and deliberately stays in the danger zone, the victim has assumed the risk and cannot recover.

Wild and domesticated animals

Owners of wild animals (e.g., reptiles, insects) are strictly liable for the harm caused by them.

Owners of domesticated animals (e.g., dogs, cats, farm animals) are only liable for their negligence regarding the animals' care and control.

An owner of a domestic animal is liable in negligence for harm caused by failure to restrain an animal, which they knew had a propensity to cause harm.

Notes for active learning

Negligence

In negligence actions, the plaintiff must prove actual, as opposed to nominal, damages caused by the defendant's negligence to prevail.

Duty to rescue

To be liable for negligence, the defendant must be under a duty to the plaintiff to avoid the risk of harm that occurred.

Generally, one has a duty to act reasonably but does not have a duty to act affirmatively to come to someone's aid from a danger that they did not create.

A duty to come to the aid of a person in danger applies for:

1) the creator of the peril,

2) someone under a contractual obligation to protect (e.g., lifeguard),

3) a close family member (e.g., parent), or

4) a nascent rescuer (i.e., initiation of rescue must reasonably continue).

Even though a person does not have an affirmative duty to come to the aid of a person in peril, once one undertakes to rescue, they must act with reasonable care.

Good Samaritan statutes in many jurisdictions exempt or limit liability, except where the defendant is grossly negligent.

A defendant who endangers themselves is liable for negligence to anyone who tries to rescue them from their misconduct.

If the defendant is not negligent in placing the victim in danger, they are not liable to an injured rescuer.

A police officer has a duty to intervene to protect citizens from criminal activity and does not have a cause of action against the citizen whose negligent conduct gave rise to the need for intervention.

General standard of conduct

Except in the circumstances prescribing a different standard of care (e.g., the standard for a minor or a skilled professional), the standard of care applicable in negligence actions is that the person must act like a reasonable adult in the circumstances.

Evidence that the defendant complied with the customs established for a customer's reasonable care is admissible but does not warrant a directed verdict for the defendant.

Statutory standard of conduct

Violation of a statute is negligence *per se* or evidence of negligence, depending on the rule in the jurisdiction, if it can be shown that:

1) the plaintiff was a member of the class whom the statute was intended to protect,

2) the harm was the type of hazard the statute was designed to protect against, and

3) the violation contributed to the harm.

While violation of a statute may be negligence *per se* or evidence of negligence, compliance with an appropriate statute is not conclusive proof of the absence of negligence.

The fact that the defendant did not possess a license required to perform the act legally is irrelevant to the proof of negligence.

Even if the defendant has violated a statute and is negligent *per se*, the defense of contributory or comparative negligence is available.

Some jurisdictions impose a gross negligence standard for a gratuitous guest suing the driver.

Standard of conduct for classes of persons

As a matter of law, children under the age of seven cannot be found to be negligent.

Parents can be held liable for the torts of their child when they fail to exercise *due care* in raising or supervising the child.

Persons acting in the role of parents can be liable for negligent supervision of children.

Method of proving fault

In tort actions based upon negligence, the trier of fact must find that the defendant is negligent by a preponderance of the evidence.

That standard of negligence is by a preponderance of the evidence is met if the plaintiff shows a probability that the defendant was negligent but is not met when the evidence only shows the possibility that the defendant was negligent.

Negligence can be proven by other means than by direct evidence.

Enough evidence concerning negligence can be proven by inference or circumstantial evidence to warrant sending the issue to the jury.

If the plaintiff died because of the defendant's conduct, and there are no living witnesses to the accident other than the defendant, the plaintiff has met their burden of producing evidence of negligence by showing that the defendant might have been negligent in causing the plaintiff's death.

To satisfy their burden of producing evidence on negligence, a plaintiff must produce expert testimony only if the jury cannot determine, based on everyday knowledge and experience, whether the defendant was negligent or whether the defendant's negligence was the cause of the plaintiff's harm.

Res ipsa loquitur

Res ipsa loquitur (Latin, *the thing speaks for itself*) is a doctrine that permits a plaintiff to offer proof that the defendant was negligent by circumstantial evidence.

If the plaintiff can offer evidence on the elements necessary to establish *res ipsa loquitur*, they have satisfied their burden of producing evidence on negligence and avoid a directed verdict.

The elements which must be proven to establish *res ipsa loquitur* are:

1) the injury to the plaintiff would not ordinarily occur in the absence of negligence and

2) the defendant was in control of the instrumentality, which caused the injury.

The plaintiff can prevail without direct proof of the defendant's negligence if they prove (or the circumstances alone indicate) that they would not have been harmed if the defendant had not been negligent.

The plaintiff need only show that it is more likely than not that the defendant was negligent and that there is a causal connection to the plaintiff's harm.

The defendant can negate the inference, which comes from the doctrine of *res ipsa loquitur,* by showing that it is just as likely that someone else's negligence caused the plaintiff's harm.

If the plaintiff attempts to prove negligence by *res ipsa loquitur*, the defendant can introduce direct evidence that they were not negligent.

Res ipsa loquitur is inapplicable in product liability cases.

Causation

The plaintiff cannot recover in tort unless the defendant's conduct is the *proximate* (i.e., legal, sufficiently related) cause of the injury.

The first issue in causation is "*but-for*" (cause-in-fact) causation.

Except in rare instances, for the plaintiff to prevail, they must prove that the harm incurred would not have occurred if the defendant had not acted in a tortuous manner.

Even if the plaintiff proves *but-for* causation, proximate cause must be proven.

The determination of proximate cause is usually a factual question for the jury to be determined by some broad guidelines.

If there is *but-for* causation, but it is determined that a separate *but-for* cause is a superseding cause, the defendant's tortious conduct is not the proximate cause of the plaintiff's harm, they cannot recover.

If the separate *but-for* cause were foreseeable by the defendant, it is not considered a superseding cause, and the plaintiff recovers.

For example, an injured plaintiff will require medical treatment.

It is foreseeable that the plaintiff will suffer additional injury from negligent medical treatment. The defendant is liable for the additional harm caused by that treatment.

The original defendant is not liable for the harm caused by a superseding intervening cause.

The original defendant is liable for harm that would have occurred if not for the superseding cause.

If the defendant has tortiously injured a plaintiff in a manner that includes a permanent disability, the plaintiff is entitled to be compensated for those injuries but not for subsequent injuries that would not have occurred if the plaintiff did not have that permanent disability.

A subsequent tortfeasor is not liable for the injuries which occurred before the time they committed the tort.

In tort actions involving damages caused to a child because of drugs taken by the pregnant mother, or in cases involving a long period between the ingestion of the dangerous substance and the injury, the ordinary tort rule that the plaintiff must prove the defendant's product caused the harm is relaxed.

Each defendant drug manufacturer will be liable for damages in proportion to the market share of the pharmaceutical the defendant had when the plaintiff consumed the item.

Allocation of liability among joint tortfeasors

Defendants are joint tortfeasors when their concurrent tortious actions combine to injure the plaintiff, and it is not possible to reasonably allocate portions of the plaintiff's injury to separate defendants.

In question where a plaintiff and defendants are alleged to be joint tortfeasors, use the following process.

1) Determine how the plaintiff's negligence affects the total amount of the award.

2) Determine how much the plaintiff can collect in damages from each defendant.

3) Determine the rights of the defendant who pays damages to collect from other defendants.

Effect of the plaintiff's negligence on damages

For *contributory negligence* jurisdictions, the plaintiff loses if negligent in any degree.

For *pure comparative negligence*, the plaintiff prevails if a defendant is negligent. However, the defendant's percentage of negligence reduces the award. A plaintiff can be 99% negligent, and the defendant 1%, the plaintiff recovers.

For *modified comparative negligence*, the plaintiff prevails *only* if the defendant's negligence is *greater* than the plaintiff's. However, the plaintiff's recovery is reduced by the percentage of their negligence.

Comparative negligence does not change the rule of jointly and severally liable between joint tortfeasors.

Amount collected from the defendant

Under common law, joint tortfeasors are jointly and severally liable for the entire judgment of the plaintiff.

If the common law has been modified, so joint tortfeasors are severally (individually) but not jointly (mutually) liable, the plaintiff can collect from each joint tortfeasor the judgment amount they are liable for.

Relations between joint tortfeasors

Under common law, a joint tortfeasor who pays more than their equal share of judgment is entitled to seek contribution from the other joint tortfeasors in the amount of any excess paid.

If the jurisdiction provides that joint tortfeasors are only liable in proportion to their percentage of negligence, a joint tortfeasor who pays more than their allocated share of the judgment is entitled to seek contribution from the other joint tortfeasors for the excess paid.

If a person is responsible for vicarious liability, they can seek indemnification from the party who is ultimately liable and collect from them the entire amount paid.

A negligent defendant is only entitled to contribution (not complete indemnification) from a negligent joint tortfeasor. A negligent tortfeasor is entitled to indemnification if a joint tortfeasor has committed an intentional tort.

Liability of owners and occupiers of land

A landowner owes a business invitee a duty to use reasonable care to prevent injuries while on the premises.

An individual is a business invitee when entering the premises intending to conduct business, whether or not they conduct it.

A landowner owes a business invitee a duty to use reasonable care to prevent the invitee from suffering from third parties' criminal acts while on the premises.

A person's status on the premises depends on the area where the injury occurs and whether the public has been invited to that area.

If the issue is the defendant's negligence because of the condition of the premises, evidence of occurrences similar to the accident in issue due to the same condition is admissible if relevant to prove that the defendant had notice of the dangerous condition.

Without incurring tort liability, a landowner can construct a legally permitted building on their land to deprive the adjoining land of light and air and remove a building on their land, which exposes the neighbor's land to sunlight.

At common law, a licensee (social guest) is only owed a duty to *warn of dangers known* to the owner or occupant but not apparent to the licensee.

Many jurisdictions have changed this rule to permit a licensee to pursue a tort claim if the landowner is negligent.

A landowner is not liable to a trespasser for ordinary negligence but is liable if they could have prevented the injury after becoming aware of the danger to the trespasser.

Attractive nuisance

At common law, a trespasser is only owed a duty to avoid gross negligence or wanton, willful misconduct.

A possessor of land is subject to liability for physical harm to children trespassing thereon caused by an artificial condition upon the land if:

1) the possessor knows or has reason to know that children are likely to trespass in the dangerous location (attractive nuisance),

2) the possessor knows or has reason to know that the condition will involve an unreasonable risk of death or serious bodily harm to such children,

3) the children, because of their youth, do not discover the condition or realize the risk involved,

4) the utility to the possessor of maintaining the proper condition and eliminating the danger is slight compared to the risk to the children involved, and

5) the possessor fails to exercise reasonable care to eliminate the danger or otherwise protect the children.

If an attractive nuisance applies, the landowner owes a duty of reasonable care to the infant trespasser(s).

The children do not need to be attracted to the land by the nuisance.

The doctrine is not applicable if the nuisance would only be attractive to those old enough to recognize its hazards.

Vicarious liability

Employers are vicariously liable for the torts of their employees committed within the scope of their employment.

An employer-employee relationship exists where the person contracting for services controls how the job is accomplished.

Indicia of an employer-employee relationship are periodic payments to the worker rather than payment by the job and ownership of the contractor's tools rather than by the worker.

The intentional tort of an employee would be within the scope of their employment if it were committed to further the master's (i.e., employer's) business even though the employer expressly forbade the conduct.

In addition to being held vicariously liable on a *respondeat superior* theory, an employer can be held liable for negligence in hiring or supervising employees.

A plaintiff injured by a servant may sue the servant and the employer.

A defendant, who has not been personally negligent and has been held vicariously liable, has a right to recover the entire amount of the judgment by indemnification from the party whose negligence caused the vicarious liability.

Parents are not vicariously liable for their children's torts but can be held liable for negligence in raising or supervising them.

Joint enterprise liability

When two persons join in accomplishing a task labeled a joint enterprise, such as participating in an automobile race, each is liable for torts committed by the other within the scope of the joint enterprise.

Liability for independent contractors

The person hiring an independent contractor is not liable for the torts of the independent contractor with the following exceptions:

The person hiring a contractor is liable for ultra-hazardous activity (e.g., blasting, pile driving) undertaken by them.

If a person has a non-delegable duty of safety for an ultra-hazardous activity, they cannot relieve tort liability by hiring an independent contractor.

A different theory of liability is that a person who hires an independent contractor can be held liable for negligence in hiring an unfit contractor.

Assumption of the risk

The assumption of the risk would be a valid defense only if the plaintiff had actual, subjective knowledge of the risk, which caused the harm, and voluntarily assumed it.

The defense of assumption of the risk will not be applicable if a defendant is in a difficult situation that they did has not cause and take reasonable effort to extricate.

The assumption of the risk is not available in product liability cases where the jurisdiction has adopted a comparative negligence doctrine applicable in product liability cases.

The assumption of the risk is combined with comparative negligence to reduce the total amount of the plaintiff's recovery.

Last clear chance

While contributory negligence bars the plaintiff's recovery, that doctrine is not applicable if the defendant had the last clear chance after the plaintiff's negligence occurred to avoid the accident.

Attribution of a related party's negligence

One party's negligence will not ordinarily be attributed to another, even for related parties.

Thus, the negligence of a minor child is not attributed to the parent, but the parent can be liable for negligent supervision of their child.

A decedent's negligence will be attributed to their executor in a wrongful death case.

Elements of tort damage

The plaintiff cannot recover in negligence without proving damage.

If an element of tort damage is future medical expenses, the plaintiff must produce expert testimony to prove the expenses expected to be incurred.

If a court determines that the defendant's tortious conduct proximately caused damages and the plaintiff's damages were not foreseeable by the defendant, this is not a valid defense.

If a tort victim is especially prone to injury, the tortfeasor must pay damages incurred because a tortfeasor takes their victim as they find them.

Economic loss to third parties caused by injuries to the defendant is not compensable as an element of tort damage.

If a tort committed on a mother before conception causes damage to a later-born child, the child could recover damages. However, there is a doubt that the child's damages are an element of the mother's damages.

Even though an employee's recovery against their employer is limited to worker's compensation, they may pursue tort claims against third parties who contributed to their injuries.

Notes for active learning

Defamation

Elements of defamation

The plaintiff must prove fault by the defendant in publishing an untrue, defamatory statement about the plaintiff.

If the plaintiff is a public figure, public official, or person well known in the field in which the defamation occurs, the plaintiff must prove that the defendant acted with *malice*; the defendant knew the statement was untrue or published it with a reckless disregard of the truth.

If the plaintiff is not a public figure, they must prove the defendant was negligent in publishing the untrue, defamatory statement.

A statement is defamatory when it might lower the esteem, in the eyes of a reputable segment of the community, of the person who is the subject of the statement.

Publication requirement

Publication of the defamatory statement is an essential element of a defamation action.

The plaintiff must prove that the defendant intended or acted in a way that it is reasonably certain that at least one person other than the plaintiff heard and understood the statement.

The publication element was satisfied even if the person receiving the defamatory statement did not believe it was true.

If a statement by the defendant is directed only to the plaintiff but is overheard by a third person, the publication issue is determined by whether the defendant should have reasonably known that the statement would be overheard.

A defendant can be liable in defamation by republishing a defamatory statement made by a third party.

Libel

Libel *per se* is a defamatory statement to anyone receiving the communication with no other information concerning the plaintiff.

Libel *per quod* is a defamatory statement only when taken in conjunction with facts known by those to whom the libel is published.

If the defamation is a writing or permanent communication (e.g., a recording), the plaintiff may prevail without proving special damages (e.g., lost profits) due to the defamation.

Humiliation, shame, or emotional distress are sufficient.

Slander

Defamation, in the form of oral communication, is slander.

An essential element of the cause of action for slander is the requirement that the plaintiff proves special damages in the form of a monetary loss caused by the defendant's defamatory statement.

The requirement of special damages is not applicable if the slander states that the plaintiff has committed a crime, has a loathsome disease, has engaged in sexual misconduct, or is incompetent in business.

Truth as defense

If the words of the communication are true as those words are reasonably construed, the defendant has a complete defense to a defamation action even if the words are not true.

Privilege as defense

Relevant statements made in a judicial proceeding are absolutely privileged, but those given in an administrative proceeding only have a qualified privilege.

Statements made by a former employer to a prospective employer concerning an employee enjoy a qualified privilege.

The defendant is liable even with a qualified privilege if they make a statement they know is false or makes a statement with reckless disregard of the truth.

Liability standard for defamation

Plaintiff	Liability standard	Damages	Burden of proof
Public official	Malice	Compensatory and punitive	Plaintiff must prove falsity of the assertion
Public figure	Malice	Compensatory and punitive	Plaintiff must prove falsity of the assertion
Private figure, (*matter of public concern*)	Negligence *and* injury	Compensatory; punitive damages require malice	Plaintiff must prove falsity of the assertion
Private figure, (*matter of private concern*)	Negligence	Compensatory; punitive damages do *not* require malice	Defendant must prove truth of the assertion

Privacy

Four invasions of privacy

The tort of invasion of privacy consists of four separate torts involving interference with a person's right to be left alone.

The four invasions of privacy torts are:

1) Unreasonable intrusion on the plaintiff's seclusion.

    The publication is not an element of this invasion of privacy.

2) Appropriation of the plaintiff's name or likeness for commercial purposes.

    The plaintiff's consent to having a picture taken does not constitute consent to use the photo for commercial purposes.

3) Unreasonable publication of the plaintiff's private life.

    The material published must be highly offensive to a reasonable person.

    Truth is not a defense to this invasion of privacy, but newsworthiness of the event in the plaintiff's private life is a defense.

    Publishing information in the public record cannot generally be considered an unreasonable invasion of the plaintiff's private life.

4) Publicity unreasonably placing another in a false light.

    The information published need not be defamatory to give rise to this form of invasion of privacy if it is untrue.

Notes for active learning

Deceit

Misrepresentation of a material fact

For the plaintiff to recover in common law deceit, there must be a misrepresentation of material fact by the plaintiff, relied upon by the defendant to their detriment.

A statement of opinion is not a misrepresentation of a material fact.

Actual damages are an essential element of a cause of action in deceit.

Failing to make a disclosure is the basis for a cause of action in deceit when there is a legal or fiduciary duty to make a disclosure.

The plaintiff must sustain more than nominal damages to have a cause of action for misrepresentation.

Third parties cannot sue for negligent misrepresentation unless the purpose of the information were to permit third parties to rely on it.

Notes for active learning

Conflict of Laws in Torts

Law of the place where the accident occurred

Lex loci delicti commissi [Latin, *the law of the place where the tort was committed*] controls.

Lex loci [Latin, *the law of the place*] applies even though the significant contacts, including the negligent act, occurred in another state.

Vicarious liability is determined by the place of the wrong only if the defendant authorized the tortfeasor to act for them in the state.

Lex loci determines the character and measure of the damages, the standard of care, causation, contributory negligence, master-servant rule, defenses, and survival of actions.

1st Restatement § 378: the law of the place of the wrong determines if there is a legal injury.

The instant the cause of action (COA) arises, the plaintiff's rights vest.

Apply the law of the place where the injury or place of wrong occurred.

This may not be the place of negligence (or other wrongs) but the place of injury.

Place of wrong – use the law of the state of consequences, not original wrong / negligence where the force impinged on the plaintiff's body.

Each state has legislative jurisdiction to determine the legal effects of acts done or events caused within a territory.

Laws of the state are intended to possess exclusive sovereignty and jurisdiction within its territory, and persons who are residents and contracts made and acts done within it:

> compensate the plaintiff for the harm they suffered,
>
> provide predictability protecting reasonable expectations of the parties,
>
> provide uniformity and administrability,
>
> discourage forum shopping.

Where harm is done to the person's reputation, the place of wrong is where the defamatory statement was communicated.

Invasion of privacy uses the law of the jurisdiction where the plaintiff was when their feelings were wounded.

Exceptions to the place of the wrong test:

1) if the wrong depends on the application of the standard of care, that standard should be taken from the law of the location of the actor's conduct;

2) a person required, forbidden, or privileged to act under the law of the "place of acting" should not be held liable for consequences on another state.

Problems with the territorial approach:

determine where the injury occurred by looking at the localizing event (e.g., reputation, trademark, mass tort case),

unfairness potential,

characterization or escape devices,

renvoi.

Establishing Agency

Agency relationships are generally formed by the mutual consent of a principal and an agent, although not always. An agency can arise as an express agency, implied agency, apparent agency, and agency by ratification. The most common form of agency is express agency. In an express agency, the agent has the authority to contract or otherwise act on the principal's behalf as expressly stated in the agency agreement. Additionally, the agent may possess certain implied or apparent authority to act on the principal's behalf.

Express agency occurs when a principal and an agent expressly agree to enter into an agency agreement with each other. Express agency contracts can be oral or written unless the Statute of Frauds stipulates that they must be written. A power of attorney is an example of an express agency. An implied agency is an agency that occurs from the parties' conduct rather than from a prior agreement between them. The facts determine the extent of the agent's authority.

Implied authority can be conferred by *industry custom*, *prior dealing between the parties*, the agent's position, and acts deemed necessary to carry out the agent's duties.

Apparent agency (or *agency by estoppel*) arises when a principal creates the appearance of an agency that does not exist. Where an apparent agency is established, the principal is estopped from denying the agency relationship and is bound to contracts entered into by the apparent agent while acting within the scope of the apparent agency. The principal's actions (not the agent's) create an apparent agency.

An *agency by ratification* occurs when a person misrepresents themself as another's agent when they are not, and the purported principal ratifies (accepts) the unauthorized act. In such cases, the principal is bound to perform, and the agent is relieved of liability for misrepresentation.

Notes for active learning

Torts – Quick Facts

Negligence:

    1)   Duty – the defendant owed a legal duty to the plaintiff

    2)   Breach of duty – the defendant breached a legal duty by acting (or failing to act) in a certain way.

    3)   Causation – the defendant's action (or failure to act) caused the plaintiff's harm.

    4)   Damages – the plaintiff was harmed or injured due to the defendant's actions (or inactions).

    A cause of action for negligence requires measurable harm to the plaintiff.

1.   The swearing of a proper complaint at the time may not serve as a basis for a **false imprisonment action** despite the failure to cancel the complaint.

2.   A landowner generally owes *no* duty to an undiscovered trespasser.

    If a landowner discovers *or* should anticipate the presence of a trespasser, the landowner *must* exercise **ordinary care** to warn the trespasser *or* make safe the concealed, unsafe, or artificial conditions *known to the landowner* that involves a risk of death or serious bodily harm.

3.   A **private nuisance** action requires a showing that the defendant's interference with the use and enjoyment of the plaintiff's property was *unreasonable.*

    A characterization of unreasonable requires that the severity of the inflicted injury *outweigh the utility* of the defendant's conduct.

4.   **Commercial invitees** are owed the duty to be warned of non-obvious dangerous conditions, and the defendant must make reasonable inspections to *discover* dangerous conditions and make them safe.

5.   The tort of **conversion** does *not* require that the defendant damage or permanently deprive the owner of the chattel – it required that the defendant's volitional conduct results in a serious invasion of the owner's chattel interest.

6.   A **bailee** is liable to the owner for conversion *if* the bailee uses the chattel in a manner that constitutes a material breach of the bailment agreement.

7.   A plaintiff can recover for defamation where there was **negligent communication** of the defamatory statements to third persons.

8. A defendant will *not* be liable to a child's parents by showing that the child *appreciated the risk* of the activity causing injury.

9. Doctors, dentists, and healthcare professionals owe their patients a duty of **informed consent** to provide the patient with information about the risks of a proposed course of treatment, surgical intervention, alternative modalities, or the election to abstain from treatment to enable the patient to make an informed decision (i.e., informed consent).

    Even if there is a **breach of duty**, there *must* be **damages.**

Relationship matrix

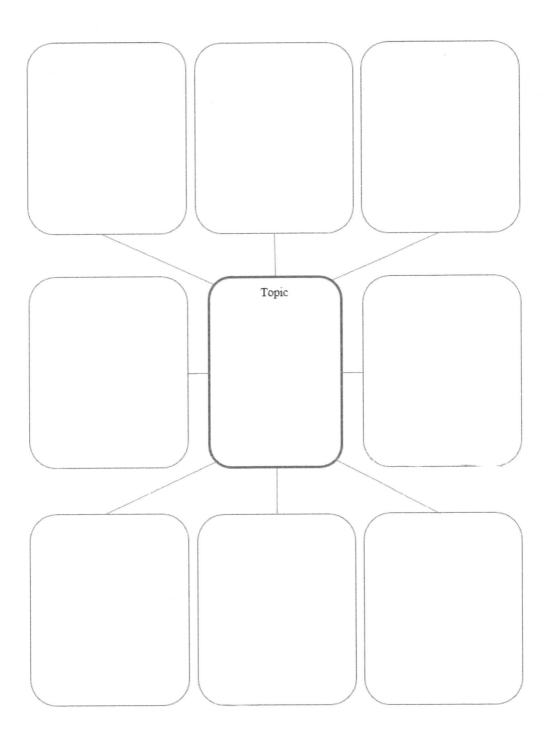

Notes for active learning

Review Questions

Multiple-choice questions

1. Who is liable when the Amazon delivery driver has an accident while delivering a package?

    I. The delivery person

    II. Amazon

    III. The manufacturer of the package

A. I only

B. I and II only

C. I and III only

D. I, II and III

2. An employee in a factory injured by their employer's negligence can sue:

A. Other employees

B. The employer

C. The worker's compensation board

D. None of the above

3. Assault is:

    I. The threat of imminent harm or offensive contact

    II. Actions arousing reasonable apprehension of imminent harm

    III. A creditor repossessing the victim's property

A. I only

B. I and II only

C. I and III only

D. III only

4. The "coming and going" rule says that principals are generally not liable for injuries caused by their agents and employees on the way to:

A. the bathroom

B. a business meeting

C. a business lunch

D. work

5. Defamation requires that:

    I. The defendant makes an untrue statement

    II. The statement is published

    III. The defendant expresses their opinion

A. I only

B. I and II only

C. II and III only

D. I, II and III

6. Examples of battery, if injury from contact, include:

      I. Threatening a person with bodily harm

      II. Throwing a dart

      III. Shooting a projectile

A. I only

B. II only

C. II and III only

D. I, II and III

7. The doctrine of proximate cause can be stated as encompassing:

A. Foreseeability

B. Damages

C. Liability

D. Negligence

8. Under the *shopkeeper's privilege*, merchants may stop, detain, and investigate suspected shoplifters without being held liable for false imprisonment if:

      I. There are reasonable grounds for the suspicion

      II. Suspects are detained for a reasonable time

      III. Investigations are conducted in a reasonable manner

A. I only

B. I and II only

C. I and III only

D. I, II and III

9. Who is liable if an Amazon delivery person punches a customer wearing an "I love Jesus" t-shirt because the delivery person hates Christians?

      I. The delivery person

      II. Amazon

      III. The T-shirt manufacturer

A. I only

B. I and II only

C. II and III only

D. I, II and III

10. *Defamation of character* requires the plaintiff to prove that:

      I. The defendant made an untrue statement of fact about the plaintiff

      II. The information included the defendant's opinion

      III. The statement was published to a third party

A. I only

B. I and III only

C. II only

D. I, II and III

11. If someone waiting for a taxi after being in an accident caused by the defendant's negligence is then hit on the head by a chipped brick falling off a high-rise building, the defendant's defense would be:

A. Superseding cause

B. Assumption of risk

C. Last clear chance

D. Comparative negligence

12. In the tort of appropriation, the plaintiff can:

I. Recover the unauthorized profits made by the offending party

II. Obtain an injunction against further unauthorized use of their identities

III. Demand defendant inform customers of the error

A. I and II only

B. II only

C. II and III only

D. I, II and III

13. The following is NOT an element of negligence:

A. A duty of care

B. Negligent conduct

C. Intent

D. Causation

14. All of the following are exceptions to the rule that a principal is not liable for the independent contractor's torts EXCEPT:

A. Nondelegable duties

B. Special risks

C. Negligence *per se*

D. Negligent selection of an independent contractor

15. Examples of the tort of *invasion of privacy* include:

I. Striking a plaintiff in the torso

II. Wiretapping

III. Searching another's personal computer

A. I and II only

B. II only

C. II and III only

D. I, II and III

16. The tort of the unlawful threat of offensive contact causing the plaintiff to believe in imminent harm is:

A. Negligent infliction of emotional distress   **C.** False imprisonment

B. Battery   **D.** Assault

17. If a hiker gets stuck under a boulder taking a selfie and the rescuer gets injured while helping, the hiker could be liable because of the:

A. Dram Shop doctrine   **C.** Social host liability doctrine

B. *Respondeat superior* doctrine   **D.** Danger invites rescue doctrine

18. In a suit for malicious prosecution, the courts require plaintiffs to prove:

    I. The plaintiff in the original lawsuit instituted the original lawsuit

    II. There was no probable cause for the initial lawsuit

    III. The plaintiff in the original lawsuit brought it with malice

A. I only   **C.** II only

B. I and II only   **D.** I, II and III

19. If a defendant intends to injure A but misses and injures B, the defendant is liable under:

A. *Respondeat superior*   **C.** Last clear chance

B. Actual malice   **D.** Transferred intent

20. The tort of *negligence* requires that the plaintiff prove that the:

    I. Defendant owed a duty of care to the plaintiff

    II. Defendant breached the duty of care

    III. Plaintiff suffered an injury

A. I and II only   **C.** I and III only

B. II only   **D.** I, II and III

21. The tort of taking another's personal property and failing to return it is:

A. Conversion   **C.** Trespass to personal property

B. False Imprisonment   **D.** Assault

22. The elements of negligence are:

    I. Duty
    II. Breach
    III. Causation

A. I and II only   **C.** II and III only
B. II only   **D.** I, II and III

True/false questions

23. Bait and switch is when a low-cost discounted item is advertised and switched for a higher-priced item.

    True   False

24. The transferred intent doctrine shifts the perpetrator's intent from the target to victim.

    True   False

25. Truth is not a defense to an invasion of privacy.

    True   False

26. Publication for defamation means published in a newspaper, magazine, or book.

    True   False

27. Opinions are often defamatory and actionable.

    True   False

28. Truth is not a defense to slander.

    True   False

29. Good Samaritan laws protect citizens who render emergency aid.

    True   False

30. People typically do not have exclusive legal rights to control and profit from the commercial use of their name and personality.

    True   False

31. Tort damages are monetary damages.

      True   False

32. False imprisonment requires that the victim be locked in jail or prison.

      True   False

33. One can commit an act of negligence without causing harm to the plaintiff.

      True   False

34. The courts look favorably on malicious prosecution lawsuits.

      True   False

35. The doctrine of *res ipsa loquitur* holds the defendant liable when the defendant's actions violated a statute designed to cover such conduct.

      True   False

36. Because of the reasonable person standard applied in negligence law, an alcoholic defendant would be held to the reasonable alcoholic standard.

      True   False

37. Assault is unauthorized and offensive contact with another person.

      True   False

38. The legal term for an oral defamatory statement is libel.

      True   False

Answer keys

1: B	11: A	21: A
2: D	12: A	22: D
3: B	13: C	
4: D	14: C	
5: B	15: C	
6: C	16: D	
7: A	17: D	
8: D	18: D	
9: A	19: D	
10: B	20: D	

23: True	31: True
24: True	32: False
25: True	33: False
26: False	34: False
27: False	35: False
28: False	36: False
29: True	37: False
30: False	38: False

Notes for active learning

Bar Exam Information, Preparation
and
Test-Taking Strategies

STERLING
Test Prep

Introduction to the Uniform Bar Examination (UBE)

Structure of the UBE

The Uniform Bar Examination (UBE) includes 1) the Multistate Bar Examination (MBE), 2) Multistate Essay Examination (MEE), and 3) Multistate Performance Test (MPT).

The MBE has 200 multiple-choice questions accounting for 50% of the UBE.

The MEE has six essays worth 30% of the UBE score.

The MPT has two legal tasks (e.g., complaint, client letter) for 20% of the UBE score.

The Multistate Bar Examination (MBE)

The Multistate Bar Examination consists of 200 four-option multiple-choice questions prepared by the National Conference of Bar Examiners (NCBE).

Of these 200 questions, 175 are scored, and 25 are unscored pretest questions.

Candidates answer 100 questions in the three-hour morning session and the remaining 100 questions in the three-hour afternoon session.

The 175 scored questions are distributed with 25 questions on each of the seven subject areas: Federal Civil Procedure, Constitutional Law, Contracts, Criminal Law and Procedure, Evidence, Real Property, and Torts.

A specified percentage of questions in each subject tests topics in those subjects.

For example, approximately one-third of Evidence questions test hearsay and its exceptions, while approximately one-third of Torts questions test negligence.

Interpreting the UBE score report

Overall score. The National Conference of Bar Examiners (NCBE) states the Uniform Bar Exam (UBE) requires a passing scaled score between 260 to 280. Scores above 280 receive a passing score in every UBE state.

The "percentile" is the number of people that scored lower. If an examinee scored in the 47th percentile, they scored higher than 47% of the examinees (and lower than 53%).

The examinee is first given a "raw score,"; based on the number of correct answers.

The raw score is adjusted by adding points to achieve the "scaled score." The number of points added is determined by a formula that compares the difficulty of the current exam to prior benchmark exams.

The comparative performance of examinees on "control questions" (prior pretest questions) given on previous exams form the basis for determining each exam's difficulty.

MBE scaled score. Examinees receive a scaled score and not an MBE "raw" score (i.e., the number of correct answers). MBE scores are scaled scores calculated by the NCBE through a statistical process used for standardized tests.

According to the NCBE, this statistical process adjusts raw scores on the current exam to account for differences in difficulty compared to previously administered exams. The scaled score is calculated from the raw score, but the NCBE does not publish the conversion formula.

Since the MBE is a scaled score, equating makes it impossible to know precisely how many questions must be answered correctly to receive a particular score. Equating allows scores from different exams to be compared since a specific scaled score represents the same level of knowledge among exams.

The MBE is curved, so just because a score is "close" to passing does not mean you are close. For example, a 124 may be in the 31st percentile and a 136 in the 62nd percentile. A 12-point difference in scaled scores equates to a 31-point percentile difference. If you are in the 120s, much preparation is needed to increase your score.

For most states, aim for a scaled score of 135 to "pass" the MBE. If you are unsure what score you need, divide the passing score by two. For example, if a 270 is needed to pass the bar, divide 268 by two to yield 135 as a threshold score on the MBE.

The importance of the MBE score

A passing MBE score depends on the jurisdiction. In jurisdictions that score on a 200-point scale, the passing score is the overall score. Passing scores are often approximately 135.

For the July 2020 bar exam, the national average MBE score was 146.1, an increase of 5 points from the July 2019 national average of 141.1.

For comparison, on the July 2018 bar, the national average MBE score was 139.5, a decrease of about 2.2 points from the July 2017 national average of 141.7.

How much the MBE contributes depends on the jurisdiction. Each jurisdiction has its policy for the relative weight given to the MBE compared to other bar exam components.

For Uniform Bar Examination (UBE) jurisdictions, the MBE component is 50%.

Most jurisdictions combine the MBE score with the state essay exam score.

The overall state candidates' performance on the MBE controls the raw state essay's conversion to scaled scores. Achieve a scaled MBE score of at least 135 to pass the bar.

MEE and MPT scores

In a UBE score report, there are six scores for the Multistate Essay Exam (MEE) and two for the Multistate Performance Test (MPT). Most states release this information.

Most states grade on a 1–6 scale (some use another scale).

In states grading on a 1–6 scale, 4 is considered a passing score.

The MEE and MPT sections are not weighted equally.

The MEE essays are worth 60%, while the MPT is 40% of the written score.

Many examinees assume that they passed the MPT and MEE portions of the exam. Examine the score report to see how you performed on these portions.

The objective of the Multistate Bar Exam

Working knowledge of the MBE objectives, the skills it tests, how it is drafted, the relationship of the parts of an MBE question, and the testing limitations provide you a substantial advantage in choosing the correct answers to MBE questions and passing the bar.

Knowing which issues are tested and the form in which they are tested makes it more manageable to learn the large body of substantive law.

The MBE's fundamental objective is to measure fairly, and efficiently which law school graduates have the necessary academic qualifications to be admitted to the bar and exceed this threshold.

The multiple-choice exam used to accomplish this objective must be of a consistent level of difficulty.

The level at which the pass decision is made must be achievable by most candidates.

The MBE tests the following skills:

- reading carefully and critically
- identifying the legal issue in a set of facts
- knowing the law that governs the legal issues tested
- distinguish between frequently confused closely-related principles
- making reasonable judgments from ambiguous facts
- understanding how limiting words make plausible-sounding choices wrong
- choosing the correct answer by intelligently eliminating incorrect choices

Notes for active learning

Preparation Strategies for the Bar Exam

An effective bar exam study plan

There are a lot of great ideas about how to prepare. Follow through with these ideas and turn them into persistent action for successful preparation.

A detailed and well-planned study schedule has benefits, such as giving you a sense of control and building confidence and proficiency.

Pick a date about 12-14 weeks before the exam (November for the February exam and April for the July exam) and use it as the start of your active study period.

Start a month earlier than many others to have a month to review as final preparation at the end.

Students have found this effective. Use an elongated prep period as a study schedule.

Most examinees prefer at least two weeks before the exam to review the material.

By planning early, you will have more time. You may want three or four final weeks to review subjects, take timed exams, and ensure that you are prepared to take the exam.

A few notes on schedule management:

> Do not *start* memorizing during your initial review period. You should be learning every week from the beginning of your study schedule. This final prep period is for reviewing and taking timed exams.
>
> If you stretch the study schedule over several months, plan review weeks into your schedule. For example, every four weeks, use a few days to review the governing law and take timed exams. This is a practical and fruitful approach as you will be more likely to retain the information.

Pick specific dates for specific tasks; this makes it more likely you will complete them.

Make sure the tasks are measurable. (e.g., practice two MEE essays).

Be realistic about the tasks, time, energy, and your ability to complete the items listed as tasks in preparation for the exam.

Remember to take some scheduled breaks from studying.

Exercise, sleep and take care of your physical and mental health.

If you are not in the right mental state preparing for the exam, you will likely be ineffective when studying and are less likely to pass the exam.

Focused studying

Some people are better at multiple-choice questions; others do better with essays.

The multiple-choice portion (MBE at 50%) and the essay portion (MEE at 30% and MPT at 20%) are weighted equally.

Doing poorly in one section means it will be challenging to achieve a passing score.

Identify weaknesses early in the preparation process and focus on them.

If you struggle with multiple-choice questions, dedicate extra time to practicing MBE questions.

If you struggle with writing, focus on completing MEE essays and complete MPT practice materials.

By reviewing your performance on released multiple-choice practice tests, be concerned if you consistently miss questions that are most answered correctly.

If you have problems with questions and perform below 50%, you lack the fundamental knowledge necessary to pass the MBE.

When reviewing your answers to practice questions, it is essential to review all questions and answers, even those you got right.

Make sure you got that correct answer for the right reason.

Reviewing the questions and answers is critical for success on the exam.

Spend time reviewing those basic principles and working deliberately on the straightforward (and easy) questions that supplement learning.

Advice on using outlines

As a user of this governing law book, several of the following points are moot. They are included, so you can be confident that you are using the proper resources to prep for the bar.

Having a useful governing law study guide (such as this book) is critical.

Without effective resources, it is challenging to understand, learn and apply the governing law to the facts given in the question.

Some students use outlines that make learning difficult.

A few common mistakes about outlines:

- Learning outlines that are too long (e.g., more than 100 pages per subject) or too short (e.g., a seven-page Contracts outline). You will be overwhelmed by information or never learn enough governing law.

- Spending too much time comparing several outlines for the same subject.

  For example, using different Contracts outlines and needlessly comparing them. This confusion results in an undue focus on insignificant discrepancies.

- Outlining every subject. If you are not starting to study early, this consumes too much study time. Do not attempt to outline all subjects. It may be a good idea to outline a select few problematic subjects.

Using a detailed and well-organized governing law outline (e.g., this book) is essential; it saves time, organizes concepts, reduces anxiety, and helps you score well and pass the bar.

Easy questions make the difference

Limitations on the examiners lead to the first important insight into preparation for the exam – the kind of questions that decide whether you pass.

Performance on specific questions correlates with success or failure on the bar.

By analyzing statistics, questions predicting success or failure have been identified.

In general, the most challenging questions were not particularly good predictors of failure because most people who missed them passed the bar.

However, many of the straightforward questions were excellent predictors of success.

The median raw score ranges from about 60% to 66% correct on the MBE.

The National Conference of Bar Examiners (NCBE) writes, "expert panelists reported that they believed MBE items were generally easy, correctly estimating that about 66% of candidates would select the right answer to a typical item."

Depending on the exam's difficulty, in most states, scoring slightly below the median (miss up to 80 questions) still passes.

The most important questions to determine if you pass are not the exceedingly challenging ones but the easy ones where 90% of the examinees answer correctly.

The easy questions usually test a basic and regularly tested point of substantive law.

The wrong choices (i.e., the distracters) are typically easy to eliminate.

Your first task in preparing for the MBE is to get easy questions correct.

Study plan based upon statistics

These statistics show that an excellent performance on either the MBE questions (approximately 67% correct) or the state essays (4s on essays) assures you a passing score.

If you fail the MBE by 9 points or the essays by 5 points, the probability of passing the bar is in the single digits.

Put effort into performing well on the MBE questions for the following reasons.

- The questions are objective, and there are enough questions that are predictable concerning content and structure that it is possible, through reasonable effort, to answer 67% of the questions correctly.

- Studying the MBE first has the added advantage of preparing the necessary substantive law for state essays.

- The essays cover several subjects, the precise topic tested is unpredictable, and the answers are graded subjectively by graders who work quickly.

You had three years of law school practice with essays and less experience with multiple-choice questions.

Master the MBE before spending time preparing for the essays.

Factors associated with passing the bar

Based on an analysis of statistics from students' performance, the following factors predict the likelihood of passing the bar:

LSAT score

First-year Grade Point Average (GPA)

LSAT scores are a significant predictor of success on the bar because the LSAT requires similar multiple-choice test-taking skills as the MBE.

The LSAT tests many of the types of legal reasoning tested on the MBE.

A lower LSAT can be overcome by a comprehensive study of the MBE governing law, but these students must work harder.

Most of the subjects tested (e.g., constitutional law, civil procedure, contracts, criminal law, real property, torts) on the MBE are taken in the first year of law school.

First-year GPA measures mastery of subjects, preparedness for exams, and the ability to understand legal principles and apply them to given fact patterns.

The MBE measures the same factors but in a multiple-choice format instead of essays.

Pass rates based on GPA and LSAT scores

Past statistics indicate that law students with LSAT scores above 155 and a first-year GPA above 3.0 are reasonably assured of passing the bar.

They should study conscientiously and take practice MBEs to perform at the level needed, but they have little cause to panic.

Students with LSAT scores between 150 and 155 and a first-year GPA between 2.5 and 3.0 are in a bit more danger of failing and need to undertake rigorous preparation.

They must achieve a scaled score of 135 and take released practice exams and understand the reasons for incorrect choices. They should prepare for state essays by learning the governing laws in this book.

Students with LSAT scores between 145 and 150 and a first-year GPA between 2.2 and 2.5 have a moderate chance of passing the bar from deliberate efforts.

These students should not rely on ordinary commercial bar reviews and need intense training, particularly on the MBE component of the bar. They must devote 50-60 hours per week for seven weeks to prepare for the bar by learning the format and content of substantive law tested on the MBE. They should take released practice exams under exam conditions and conscientiously study the questions missed.

Students with LSAT scores below 145 and a GPA below 2.2 have had a failure rate of approximately 80%.

They must prep faithfully and conscientiously beyond the advice above and must engage in a rigorous course of study, more than is demanded by a traditional bar review course.

Notes for active learning

Learning and Applying the Substantive Law

Knowledge of substantive law

The fundamental reason for missing a question is 1) a failure to know the principle of law controlling the answer or 2) failure to understand how that principle is applied.

You must know and apply the governing law to pass the bar. If you do not know the governing law, you will not apply it to answer correctly.

Many students *think* they understand the governing law but do not know the nuances. Do not assume that you understand the governing (i.e., substantive) law. It is prevalent for students not to know the governing law well.

Re-learn the substantive and procedural law taught in first-year courses.

A major mistake is not to memorize the governing law outlined in this book.

The multiple-choice and essay portions test nuances and details of governing law. It is essential to analyze the governing law as it is applied in the context of the question.

On the multiple-choice section, many questions require fine-line distinctions between similar principles of law.

Several multiple-choice answers will *seem* correct, given the limited time to answer. If your knowledge of the governing law is suboptimal, you will not make these subtle distinctions and will have to guess on many questions.

For the essay to be developed, you must know the governing law and apply it to the issues within the call of the question.

If you do not know the governing law, you will not state the correct rule in your essay. You will be unable to apply the correct rule to the fact pattern.

Where to find the law

The questions must be related to the subject matter outlined in the bar examiners' (NCBE) materials.

While the NCBE outline is broad and ambiguous, years of experience with the exam delineate the scope of material you must learn.

The governing law covered in this book is foundational to the exam. The governing law statements were compiled by analyzing questions released by the multistate examiners. The analysis revealed a limited number of legal principles repeatedly tested.

Review these principles before taking practice exams and understand how they are applied to obtain the correct answer.

The property questions are probably the most difficult. The fact patterns are usually long and involve many parties in complex transactions.

In preparing for the exam, learn basic property principles and apply them. However, extensive studying into property law's crevices is not necessary to score well on these questions.

Feel confident that you do not have to go beyond the information provided in this book to find the governing law.

Controlling authority

The examiners have specified the sources of authority for the correct answers.

In Constitutional Law and Criminal Procedure, it is Supreme Court decisions.

In Criminal Law, it is common law.

In Evidence, the Federal Rules of Evidence controls.

In Torts and Property, it is the generally accepted view of United States law.

The UCC is the controlling authority in sales (Article 2) questions.

The NCBE released questions, and the published answers determine the controlling law through deduction.

Recent changes in the law

The exam is prepared months before it is given because of logistical requirements. Therefore, the examiners cannot incorporate recent changes in the law into the questions.

Recent changes in the law will not form the basis for correct answers.

If a recent change makes an answer initially designated as the correct answer to be incorrect, the examiners will credit more than one answer.

The recent holding of a Supreme Court case will not be tested for about two years since the decision was published.

Lesser-known issues and unusual applications

Some of the challenging exam questions are based on obscure principles of law.

Missing the most challenging questions will not cause you to fail the exam if you have a solid understanding of the governing law. You can learn these principles and answer the question correctly, thereby improving your overall performance.

There are instances where the correct answers are different from the usual rules.

For example, hearsay evidence inadmissible at trial is admissible before a judge hearing evidence on a preliminary question of fact (e.g., Federal Rules of Evidence 104(a)).

Practice applying the governing law

Some students know the governing law but have problems *applying* it to the facts.

The exam is as much about testing skills as it is about testing the governing law.

Therefore, knowledge of the governing law is not enough to pass.

You must practice answering multiple-choice questions and writing well-organized, coherent, and complete essays where you apply the governing law to the given facts.

Know which governing law is being tested

A typical wrong answer (i.e., distracter) on a question is an answer which is correct under a body of law other than the governing law being tested.

An example is a question governed by Article 2 of the Uniform Commercial Code (UCC), where an offer is irrevocable if:

1) it is in writing,

2) made by a merchant, and

3) states that it is irrevocable.

One of the wrong answers states the correct rule under the common law of contracts, where an offer is revocable unless consideration is paid (i.e., an option) for the promise to keep it open.

Answers which are always wrong

Some commonly used distracters are always wrong and can be eliminated quickly.

For example, a choice in an evidence question says, "character can only be attacked by reputation evidence." This choice is wrong because both opinion and reputation evidence is admissible under the Federal Rules of Evidence when character attacks are permissible.

Honing Reading Skills

Reading skills are critical. The basic level is reading to understand the facts, identify the issue and keep the parties distinct. A mistake at this juncture results in answering incorrectly, no matter how much law is known.

Understanding complex transactions

If the question involves a transaction with many parties, diagram the transaction before analyzing the choices.

The diagram should show the relationship between the parties (e.g., grantor-grantee, assignor-assignee), the transaction date, and the person's relationships in the transaction (e.g., donee, *bona fide* purchaser).

Impediments to careful reading

Two reasons candidates fail to read carefully are:

1) hurrying through a question,

2) fatigue due to a lack of sleep or strain caused by the exam.

A careful test taker maintains a steady, deliberate pace during the exam. Practice in advance and be well-rested on the test day.

Reading too much into a question

The examiners are committed to designing questions, which are "a fair index of whether the applicant has the ability to practice law." Psychometric experts ensure that they are fair and unbiased.

Even though you must read every word of these carefully drafted questions, do not read the question to find some bizarre interpretation.

The examiners must ask fair questions and not rely on "tricks." Reading too much into a question and looking for a trick lurking behind every fact leads to the wrong answer often.

It is the straightforward questions that determine whether you pass, not the occasional challenging question that tests some arcane principle of law.

Therefore, take questions at face value.

Read the call of the question first

Before reading the facts, read the call of the question because it indicates the task for selecting the correct answer. This perspective focuses your attention before reading the facts.

The question contains many *words of art*, such as "most likely," "best defense," or "least likely," which govern the correct answer.

The call is often phrased positively; the "best argument" or "most likely result."

Read answers for consistency with the question and eliminate inconsistent choices.

Negative calls

When the call of the question is negative, asking for the "weakest argument" or asking which of the options is "not" in a specified category, examine each option with the perspective that the choice with those negative characteristics is the correct answer.

After reading and understanding the question stem, read the call of the question again before reading the choices.

Analyze each choice with the requirements specified in the call of the question.

Read all choices

Never pick an answer until carefully reading all the choices. The objective is to pick the best answer, which cannot be determined until comparing the choices.

Sometimes the difference between the right and wrong answer is that one choice is more detailed or precisely sets forth the applicable law. You do not know that until reading all the answers carefully.

Broad statements of black letter law may be correct

When reading an answer, do not rule out choices with imprecise statements of the applicable *black letter* law.

If the examiners always included a choice that was precisely on point, the questions would be too easy. Instead, they often disguise the wording used in the correct answer.

For example, the Federal Rules of Evidence contain an elaborate set of relevancy rules that limit the right to introduce evidence of repairs after an accident. If there was a question where the introduction of that evidence was permissible, and no choices specifically cite the exception to the general rule of exclusion, an answer phrased with the general rule of relevancy "Admissible because its probative value outweighs its prejudicial effect," would be the correct answer.

Multiple-Choice Test-Taking Tactics

Determine the single correct answer

Increase the odds of picking the correct answer based on technical factors independent of substantive (governing) law knowledge.

The examiners' limitation is that every question must have one demonstrably correct and three demonstrably incorrect answers, limiting how the examiners write the choices.

From the question's construction, this limitation may give clues about the answer.

Process of elimination

Answering a multiple-choice question is not finding the ideal answer to the question asked but instead picking the best option.

Eliminate choices and evaluate the remaining choice for plausibility.

Eliminate choices that state an incorrect proposition of law or do not relate to the facts.

If you eliminate three options and the remaining one is acceptable, pick it and move on.

Elimination increases the odds

It takes about 125 correct answers to pass the MBE. An important strategy in reaching that number is intelligently eliminating choices.

If you are sure of the answer to only 50 of the 200 questions on the exam and confidently eliminate two of the four choices on the remaining 150 questions. Guess between the two remaining choices, and the odds predict 75 correct.

Those 75 correct, coupled with 50 questions you were confident of the answer, produce a raw score of 125 on the MBE and a scaled score above the benchmark 135.

Unfortunately, you cannot avoid guessing on questions, but intelligent methods reduce options to only two viable choices.

Sometimes you might not be able to eliminate the wrong answers just because you are sure of the answer to one of the choices. Eliminating with confidence even one choice increases the probability of correctly answering the question.

Eliminating two wrong answers

Specific questions on the MBE are challenging because of distinguishing between two choices when selecting the best answer.

A typical comment from examinees leaving the exam is, "I could not decide between the last two choices."

The positive side of that problem is eliminating two of the four choices.

Pick the winning side

The most common choice pattern is the "two-two" pattern – two choices state that the plaintiff prevails, and two that the defendant prevails.

The best approach for this type of question is to rely on your knowledge of the law or instinctive feeling to which conclusion is correct.

In a question with two choices on one side and two on the other side of a court's decision, first, pick a choice on the side you think should prevail.

Distinguish between the explanations following this conclusion and pick the choice that best justifies it.

Distance between choices on the other side

If the justifications following the conclusion for the side you chose seem indistinguishable, look at the explanations for the choices on the other side.

If the reasons for the choices on the other side are readily distinguishable, and one appears reasonable and the other incorrect, reconsider your initial conclusion.

Remember, the examiner is required to provide a distinguishable reason why one explanation of a general conclusion is correct, and the other is wrong.

That obligation does not exist if the general conclusion itself is incorrect.

Suppose choices (A) and (B) on one side look correct; that is, they are reasonable and consistent with the fact pattern. One of the choices with the opposite conclusion, answer (C), seems incorrect or inconsistent with the facts, and answer (D) with the same general conclusion sounds reasonable. From a strictly technical viewpoint, the best choice is answer (D).

Questions based upon a common fact pattern

There are several instances where two or more questions are based on the same facts.

Look at the second question's wording to guide the first question's correct answer. When asked to assume an answer to a first question from a fact pattern to answer the second question, the probability is high that the answer to the first question follows that assumption.

For example, if the first question has two choices beginning with "P prevails" and two with "D prevails," and the second question starts with "If P prevails," it is likely one of the "P prevails" choices is correct for the first question. If you picked "D prevails," think carefully before selecting it as the final answer.

Multiple true/false issues

In addition to true/false questions, the exam sometimes states three propositions in the root of the question and tests characteristics of those propositions in the call of the question.

The choices list various combinations of propositions.

The difference between this type of question and the double true/false question is that only four of the eight possible combinations fit into the options. It is possible to answer correctly even if you are not sure of all propositions' truth or falsity but are sure of one.

Correctly stated, but the inapplicable principle of law

The task of the examiners is to make the wrong choices look attractive. A creative way to accomplish this is to write a choice that impeccably states a rule of law that is not applicable because of facts in the root of the question.

For example, in a question where a person is an assignee, not a sublessee, one of the choices may correctly state the law for sublessees, but it is inapplicable to the fact pattern.

Therefore, these answer choices with inapplicable law can be confidently eliminated.

"Because" questions

Conjunctions are commonly used in the answers. It is essential to understand their role in determining whether a choice is correct.

The word "because" connects a conclusion and the reason for that conclusion with the facts in the body of the question.

There are two requirements for a question using "because" to be correct:

1) the conclusion must be correct,

2) the reasoning must logically follow based upon facts in the question, and the statement which follows "because" must be legally correct.

If the "because" choice has the correct result for the wrong reason, it is incorrect.

"If" questions

The conjunction "if" requires a much narrower focus than "because."

When a choice contains an "if," determine whether the entire statement is true, assuming that the proposition which follows the "if" is true.

There is no requirement that facts in the root of the question support the proposition following "if." There is no requirement for facts in the question to support the proposition that such a construction be reasonable.

"Because" or "if" need not be exclusive

There is no requirement for the conclusion following "if" or "because" to be exclusive.

For example, if a master could be liable in tort under the doctrine of _respondeat superior_ or because the master was _negligent_, a choice using "if" or "because" holding the master liable would be correct if it stated either reason, even though the master might be liable for the other reason.

Exam tip for "because"

Notice that in an answer that would have been correct, the word "because" limits the facts you could consider to those in the body of the question containing specific facts.

The difference between the effect of "if" and "because" controls the answer.

Identify those limited situations (e.g., where the appropriate standard is strict liability) and distinguish them from those that are satisfactory (e.g., if the standard is negligence).

"Only if" requires exclusivity

Sometimes the words "only if" are used to distinguish between the two "affirmed" choices to make one wrong.

When an option uses the words "only if," assume that the entire proposition is correct as long as the words following "only if" are true.

The critical difference, where "only if" is used, is that the proposition cannot be true except when the condition is true. If there is another reason for the same result to be reached, the choice is wrong.

"Unless" questions

The conjunction "unless" has the same function as "only if," except that it precedes a negative exclusive condition instead of a positive exclusive condition.

It is essentially the mirror image of an "only if" choice.

For an option using "unless," reverse and substitute the words "only if" for "unless."

Limiting words

Choices can be made incorrect with limiting words that require that a proposition be true in all circumstances or under no circumstances.

Examples of limiting words include *all*, *any*, *never*, *always*, *only*, *every*, and *plenary*.

Notes for active learning

Making Correct Judgment Calls

Applying the law to the facts

Most questions give a fact pattern and ask which choice draws the correct legal conclusion required by the call of the question.

The first skill required is to draw inferences from facts given to place the conduct described in the question in the appropriate legal category.

The second skill is to apply the appropriate legal rule to conduct in that category and choose the option which reaches the appropriate conclusion.

The process of drawing inferences from a fact pattern and placing conduct in an appropriate category often requires judgment.

Bad judgment equals the wrong answer

To make the questions difficult, the examiners often place the conduct near the border of two different legal classifications.

Decide which side of the demarcation the conduct falls on. Inevitably, reasonable people can differ on these judgments.

If your judgment does not match the examiners, you will likely answer the question incorrectly, no matter how much law you know.

Mitigate this problem by reviewing released questions involving judgment calls where the examiners have published correct answers (i.e., their judgment call).

For example, a death occurring because the parties played Russian roulette is considered *depraved heart murder*, not *involuntary manslaughter*.

Judgment calls happen

Difficult judgment calls occur several times on the exam, and you are likely to make some close judgment calls incorrectly.

While this adds to the frustrations of multiple-choice tests, it is part of the exam.

By narrowing judgment call questions to two choices and guessing, you will get approximately half of them correct.

You will not fail the exam solely because you were unlucky on judgment calls.

The examiners remove many judgment calls by procedural devices.

The importance of procedure

The question may not ask what a jury should find on the facts.

The answer may be controlled by the procedural context of the criminal prosecution.

For example, it is given that the jury has found the defendant guilty of murder, and the only question on appeal is whether the judge should have granted a motion to dismiss at the end of hearing evidence. This is because a reasonable jury looking at the facts and inferences most favorable to the prosecution should not have found the defendant guilty of murder.

The same procedural issues exist when the question asks if a motion for summary judgment should be allowed or if the court should direct a verdict.

Exam Tips and Suggestions

Timing is everything

The time given to complete the exam is usually adequate if you practiced enough questions to improve speed and efficiency to the required level.

As you get closer to the test date, just doing practice questions is not enough.

You need to time your practice. Take previously released exams in two three-hour periods on the same day. Since these practice exams are approximately the same length as the exam, you will know if you have a timing problem.

If you do not practice under timed conditions, you risk exhausting time on the exam before answering all the questions.

Practice your timing under test-like conditions to know if the timing will be an issue. If you cannot complete the practice exam, you will have trouble with the exam.

If time is an issue, adjust your pace and continue practicing.

All questions do not require the same amount of time.

An approach for when time is not an issue

If you can complete 100 questions in three hours, use this strategy. At the start of the exam, break the allotted time into 15-minute intervals and write them down.

Set an initial pace of 9 questions every fifteen minutes.

Check your progress at each 15-minute interval.

If you completed 18 questions in the first half-hour, 36 in the first hour, 72 in the first two hours, and 90 in the first two and a half hours, you are on target to complete the exam on time. At this pace, you should complete 100 questions in two hours and forty-six minutes.

This leaves 14 minutes to check the answer sheet, revisit troublesome questions, or use the time to go a little slower on the last questions when fatigue impairs acuity.

If you find that your careful pace is faster than the budgeted 9 questions every 15 minutes, work at a faster pace, but use the extra time on the more challenging questions or in rechecking your work at the end.

Do *not* change the original answer choice unless you have a specific reason.

It is unwise to leave the exam early.

An approach for when time is an issue

During practice, continue answering questions to complete the section even after the time for self-paced exams has expired. Note which question you completed within the allocated time. Strive to complete the questions within the allotted time during your final exam prep.

If you learn from taking the practice test that you may not finish the questions in the allotted time on the actual exam, skip those questions with a long fact pattern followed by only one question. Keep your place on the answer sheet by skipping the row.

Return to those questions at the end and complete as many as time permits. Before turning your exam in, guess at the rest to reduce the number of random guesses.

Answer every question, even if you have not read the question, since wrong answers do *not* count against you.

Difficult questions

If you do not know the answer, do not spend a disproportionate amount of time on it since each question counts the same. Mark it in the test booklet, make a shrewd guess within the budgeted time and come back if time allows.

Do *not* leave questions unanswered. No points are deducted for wrong answers.

Minimize fatigue to maximize your score

The mental energy required to answer all the multiple-choice questions under stress produces fatigue (even with a lunch break).

Fatigue slows processing questions effectively and impairs reading comprehension. You may process questions more slowly at the end of each session and more quickly at the beginning before fatigue sets in.

Take at least two released exams under timed conditions to know how significantly fatigue affects your performance.

Be sure to arrive at the exam site on time. If necessary, stay at a nearby hotel rather than getting up early and risking a long drive the morning of the exam.

Relax during the lunch break and do not discuss the morning session with others.

You should know enough about your metabolism to eat the correct foods during the exam and reinforce appropriate caffeine levels if appropriate.

Proofread the answer sheet

As you decide on each correct answer, circle the corresponding letter in the exam book, and mark the appropriate block on the answer sheet.

The answer sheet is the only document graded by the examiners.

At the pace of 9 questions per 15 minutes, about 14 minutes should remain. Spend that time proofreading the answer sheet. Verify the answers circled to be certain that you marked the appropriate block on the answers.

Ensure that there are no blanks, and no questions have two answers.

Do *not* use this time to change an answer already selected unless you have a particularly good reason to change it.

If you have erased, ensure the erasure is thorough, or the computer may reject the answer because it cannot distinguish between marked answers.

If you have time after proofreading, review the problematic questions, and re-think the answers chosen. However, even after careful thought, hesitate to change an answer.

Do not leave any section of the exam early; use the allotted time wisely.

Intelligent preparation over a sustained period

There is no easy way to conquer an exam as challenging and comprehensive as the MBE, except through practice and an investment of time and effort well before the exam.

By diligently preparing, practicing questions, and intelligently assessing why questions were answered incorrectly, your skills for the exam will improve substantially.

Continue to improve those skills by following the advice given herein until reaching a proficiency level enabling you to pass the bar. This proficiency is accurately measured in multiple-choice format questions.

Some students will have to work harder to achieve the required proficiency.

The tools are in this study guide, and any law school graduate can be successful in passing the bar if they invest the required time and effort to be prepared.

Notes for active learning

Essay Preparation Strategies and Essay-Writing Suggestions

Memorize the law

Do not make the mistake of waiting too long before memorizing the governing law. Start learning the governing law early to be better prepared and pass the exam.

Memorize essential principles and focus on highly tested governing law.

Focus on the highly tested essay rules

Do not treat all subjects the same when you prepare for the essay portion of the exam.

Some governing law topics are tested more than others. It is crucial to focus on the highly tested topics (e.g., torts, contracts. property, civil procedure).

Know and apply enough governing laws to pass the bar – focus on commonly tested governing laws (e.g., negligence) provided in this book.

Practice writing essay answers each week

Practicing is crucial to a high score on essays. Practice regularly and avoid procrastination for this essential component of bar prep.

Incorporate practicing essay writing into your exam study schedule. To reduce procrastination, schedule time for writing practice essays each week.

For the MPT, practice by drafting full MPTs. Most examinees procrastinate on preparing for the MPT; there is nothing to memorize.

Do not make the *fatal mistake* of not practicing. The MPT portion is worth 20% of the UBE score.

Know the format and *practice that format to* increase your UBE score. This practice will increase your score and the probability of passing the bar.

Add one essay-specific subject each week

The Multistate Essay Exam (MEE) subjects include the 7 MBE subjects plus the 5 subjects of Business Associations (Agency, Partnerships, Corporations, and LLCs), Conflict of Laws, Family Law, Trusts and Estates, and Secured Transactions (UCC Article 9).

Combine highly tested subjects (e.g., torts) with less-tested subjects (e.g., secured transactions) and complex topics (e.g., contracts) with easier topics (e.g., business associations).

From preparation, know which subjects you struggle with and require a focused effort to master the essential governing law.

Make it easy for the grader to award points

Your answer to a question will probably be read in less than five minutes by a grader with a checklist to find that you have seen the issues and discussed them intelligently. Writing organized and clear answers makes it easy for the essay grader to award points.

Use headings for each of the major issues.

If the question suggests a structure for the answer because it is divided into parts or because the facts present a series of discrete issues, use the structure of the question, which is probably the structure of the checklist.

Use the IRAC method for the essay questions: state the issue, state the Rule. Apply the rule to the facts and conclude. IRAC seems simple, but following this approach makes it easier for the grader to know that you identified and addressed every issue and applied the law to the facts given.

IRAC results in more points during the exam.

Do not spend time trying to formulate eloquent issue statements. The question often outlines the issues, so an eloquent issue statement is redundant, and issue statements do not earn extra points.

Many examinees spend too much time developing an impressive issue statement and omit other essentials of their analysis (e.g., truncated analysis section).

An issue statement "Torts" or "Is the defendant liable for negligence?" is enough.

Do not waste time arguing both sides. There are no "two sides" for many essays to argue on bar essays because these are not law school essays.

Apply the law to facts and conclude unless asserting each party has good arguments.

Conclusion for each essay question

Points will be lost unless you conclude for each issue identified in the facts or are asked to address it in the call of the question.

Use caution starting the essay with the conclusion unless confident it is correct.

Many sample answers provided by the National Conference of Bar Examiners start with a definite and strong conclusion. Use caution to start with a conclusion unless confident (e.g., NCBE sample responses) your conclusion is correct.

Starting with a conclusion that is not correct draws attention to an incorrect conclusion at the start, which may influence the grader disproportionality. The grader may lose faith in your answer from the onset, and it is advisable to have a neutral heading rather than a firm conclusion that is wrong.

Tips for an easy-to-read essay

Use paragraph breaks between the Issue, Rule, Analysis, and Conclusion. Paragraph break makes it easy for the grader to read and score your essays. Additionally, this approach makes the answer appear longer and more complete.

Emphasize keywords and phrases. Underline key phrases so the grader notices that you addressed the governing law and applied it to the facts given.

After graders score several essays on the same topic, they scan essays for specific phrases that they expect to locate within a complete essay.

Think before you write

Read each question carefully to understand the facts and their necessary implications thoroughly and accurately.

After skimming the question, spend time on the focus line at the end of the question. Review the facts with the call of the question in mental focus.

Write a short outline of the issues raised. Outline in your mind the issues; state to yourself the tentative conclusions; test each conclusion from the standpoints of law and common sense; revise, as necessary.

Decide on a logical, orderly, and convincing arrangement for the response. Until then, you are not ready to write the answer.

Of the thirty-six minutes allotted to each essay, spend 15 minutes on issue spotting and organization and about twenty minutes writing the answer.

The ability to think and communicate like a lawyer

The Board knows that you have completed law school, under competent instructors, and have passed law school exams. The bar does not challenge the results of your law school courses.

The exam tests the ability to apply what you have learned to facts that might arise in practice and which, in some instances, involve several fields of law. The value of an answer depends not only on the correctness of the conclusions but on displaying essential legal principles and thinking like a lawyer.

Conclude on each issue presented. If a conclusion is derived from fuzzy facts, construct a well-reasoned argument supporting your conclusion to receive full credit regardless of if you conclude the same as the examiners.

If the correct answer depends on a provision of substantive law, which you are not familiar with, you can obtain a passing answer to the question by reaching a well-reasoned conclusion applying general law principles.

Do not try to limit the question to a particular subject area. Many questions combine traditional subjects, and you must be prepared to answer the question applying principles you learned across various subjects.

Do not restate the facts

The examiners know the facts; there is no time to waste. Do not restate the facts but use them to apply and integrate legal principles in writing the essay.

Do not fight the facts, particularly the focus line of the question.

For example, if the facts state that A executed a valid will, write about valid wills. If the question asks you to argue on behalf of A, do not argue on behalf of B because B has a prevailing argument. However, raise potential arguments which could be made on behalf of B and counter them in arguing on behalf of A.

Do not state abstract or irrelevant propositions of law

It is usually undesirable to begin an answer with a legal proposition. If the proposition is applicable, it will be more appropriate later to indicate the reason for your conclusion. If it is not applicable, do not state a surplus fact or legal principle.

Although it is seldom necessary to state an applicable rule of law in detail, make a sufficient reference to it so that the examiner appreciates your knowledge of the principle and conditions when it applies.

Do not, by speculating on different facts, nor in other ways, work into your answer some point of law with which you happen to be familiar, but which does not apply to the answer. Importantly, the examiners are not interested in knowing how many rules of law you know, but your ability to apply the applicable rules to the facts.

If the question says that A and B in the above hypothetical are unrelated, do not talk about the results which would occur if they were husband and wife.

Use the principles of law applicable to the call of the question and the facts. You must state the principles of applicable law to demonstrate to the examiner that you know the elements of the rule and how they apply to these facts.

For example, if the facts said that A transferred to B (a non-relative) the money necessary for B to purchase Blackacre from C and asks who owns Blackacre, you would say, "Since A furnished the consideration for the purchase of Blackacre and B took the title to the property in their name, B holds title to Blackacre in a resulting trust for A.

Do not detail the black letter law of resulting trusts since you have shown your knowledge by properly applying the facts to the law of resulting trusts.

Do not fight the facts and address a contrary fact not presented. The examiners may take points away if you make that mistake because you are not focused on the issues presented.

Discuss all the issues raised

A grasp of all the issues is essential.

For example, if there are three issues in a question, a discussion of only one issue, no matter how masterly, if coupled with omitting the others, could not result in 100% credit. It would probably result in a score of 33%.

The exam includes many issues in most questions so it can be graded mechanically. This maintains consistency across a group of several graders for each exam question.

The grader has a checklist of issues and awards most points for the examinee that identifies issues and intelligently discusses each.

Failure to see and discuss enough issues intelligently is probably the biggest reason for failure on the essay portion of the exam.

Methods for finding all issues

Use all the facts presented. Failure to discuss facts probably means that you missed important issues.

If you must decide in the early part of the question (e.g., does the court have jurisdiction) and you decide that issue so the remaining facts become irrelevant, make an alternative assumption ("If the court does have jurisdiction") and answer the question in the alternative using facts which would otherwise be irrelevant.

Do not avoid issues because you are not sure of the substantive law. If the examiners stated that X's nephew helped X escape after a crime, discuss the nephew's status as an accessory after the fact. If you do not know whether he is a close enough relative to be exempt under the statute, answer this issue by making alternative assumptions.

Indicators requiring alternative arguments

Ambiguous terms – if there are words in the fact pattern that are neutral or ambiguous such as "put up," the examiners look for possible interpretations of these terms.

Language in quotes – language placed in quotes is almost always ambiguous and must be construed as part of the answer.

Avoid ambiguous, rambling statements and verbosity

Generally, do not use compound sentences. Two separate sentences are preferred.

Complex sentences are particularly useful to apply the facts of the question to the applicable principle of law.

For example, in the previous resulting trust hypothetical, write, "Since B purchased Blackacre and took title in their name with money furnished by A, A holds title to Blackacre in a resulting trust, even if B has not signed a memorandum."

Avoid undue repetition

If the same principle of law and conclusion apply to two parts of an answer, state it once in detail, and refer back for the second part.

For example, if you have discussed A's liability and now must discuss B's liability, say, "B is also guilty of murder for the same reasons as A. (see discussion above)."

Avoid slang and colloquialism

The examiners judge your formal writing style.

If the examiner shows humor with names and events, do not show your sense of humor.

Use the standard abbreviations:

P for Plaintiff

D for Defendant

K for Contract

BFP for *Bona Fide* purchaser

Write legibly and coherently

Printing is usually easier to read than handwriting.

Use all the pages, and do not crowd your answer.

Plan your answer so that you do not have to use inserts and arrows.

Timing strategies

On the MEE, you must complete six equally weighted essay questions in three hours; an average of 30 minutes per question.

You have flexibility with time limitations as questions are not of the same difficulty.

There are two absolute figures:

spend no more than 45 minutes on any question,

spend at least 20 minutes on each question.

Be careful about not going over the time limit on the first question because this will require a readjustment of your timing for the entire session. If you miss the deadlines, re-divide your remaining time so that you will have an equal amount of time on each question.

If you go over by 15 minutes a question, do not allocate 30 minutes for other questions.

Stay focused

Do not start by reading the entire exam. Answer the questions in order and do not consider more than one question at a time.

After answering, put it out of your mind and not worry about your response. Keep your mind clear to focus on the next question.

Proofread your answers as time permits.

Law school essay grading matrix

An "A" answer is an outstanding response. It correctly and fully identifies dispositive issues and sub-issues raised by the question. The answer states the applicable legal rules and sub-rules with precision. It analyzes the question thoroughly with the applicable rules and explores alternative analysis where appropriate. It applies the law to the facts to conclude and is not cluttered by irrelevant matters. An "A" answer demonstrates an objectively superior mastering of the subject. An answer is not an "A" answer simply because it is better than most students' answers.

A "B" answer is a good response. It presents the four components of a good answer (issues, rules, analysis & application, and conclusion), but it does so in a way that could be improved. For example, it may be that not all critical issues have been spotted, or the issues are not presented clearly. The statement of legal rules captures that basic law but may not develop the law's complexities or nuances. The analysis is competent but lacks subtlety and may be somewhat simplistic or conclusory.

A "C" answer is a minimally competent response. It contains the four components of a good answer (issues, rules, analysis & application, and conclusion) but may not distinguish them. Perhaps only some issues have been identified while others are missed. The rules of law lack completeness or accuracy. The analysis and application may be shallow and conclusory. Conclusions may be questionable and not well-defended.

A "D" answer lacks basic components. It may identify the wrong issues or none. Rules are stated incorrectly. The analysis is conclusory or absent. The law is not applied to the facts coherently. Conclusions are unsupported or missing. The response exhibits a lack of knowledge of legal issues and rules or demonstrates an inability to engage in legal analysis.

Best wishes with your preparation!

Appendix

Negligence

Negligence is a legal theory that must be proved before another can be held legally responsible for the harm suffered. Proving negligence is required in most claims from accidents or injuries (e.g., car accident, slip and fall).

Negligence claims must prove four things in court: duty, breach, causation, and damages/harm.

When a person acts carelessly and causes an injury to another, the careless person will be liable for the resulting harm under the legal principle of negligence. This basis for assessing and determining fault is used in disputes involving injury, informal settlement talks, and personal injury trials.

Elements of negligence

To prevail in a negligence action, the plaintiff must prove four elements if the defendant acted negligently:

1. Duty – the defendant owed a legal duty to the plaintiff;

2. Breach – the defendant breached that legal duty by acting (or failing to act) in a certain way;

3. Causation – it was the defendant's actions (or lack of action) that caused the plaintiff's injury; and

4. Damages – the plaintiff was harmed due to the defendant.

#1: Duty

When assessing a negligence claim, consider whether the defendant owed the plaintiff a legal *duty of care*. Duty may arise from familial relationships, contracts (e.g., lifeguard), placing the plaintiff in danger or initiating, but aborting, rescue. For example, a physician owes a patient a legal duty to provide them with competent medical care.

#2: Breach of duty

The court evaluates whether the defendant breached a duty by doing (or not doing) something that a *reasonably prudent person* would do under similar circumstances.

The reasonably prudent person is a legal standard of responsible behavior in a particular situation.

For example, the defendant will be held liable in negligence if the average person, knowing what the defendant knew at the time, would have known that someone might have been injured due to their actions and would have acted differently than the defendant.

#3: Causation

The plaintiff must prove that the defendant's negligence caused their injury. Causation determines whether the defendant could reasonably have foreseen that their actions (or lack of) might cause an injury. If the defendant's actions caused the plaintiff injury through an unexpected act of nature, the injury would be deemed unforeseeable, and the defendant not liable.

#4: Damages

The final element of negligence is "damages," requiring the court to compensate the plaintiff for their injury, usually through monetary compensation for expenses (e.g., medical care, property repair).

The reasonable person

To be negligent is to act (or fail to act) in a way that causes injury to another. What distinguishes a common accident from negligence is the *standard of care* required. By neglecting the proper standard of care, an individual may be found liable for resulting injuries.

For example, a motorist must exercise the same care that a "reasonable person" would, including obeying traffic laws and paying attention to pedestrians and other drivers. If a severely nearsighted driver who forgets to wear their glasses hits a jaywalking pedestrian, they would be negligent because a reasonable, severely nearsighted person would not drive without eyewear.

Injury claims

The *reasonable person* is a legal fiction. Such a "person" is an ideal, focusing on how a typical person with prudence would act. The test as to whether a person has acted as a reasonable person is an objective one; it does not consider specific abilities. Thus, a person chronically careless or with impaired cognitive capacity is held to the same standard as a careful person or a person of higher aptitude.

A jury generally decides whether a defendant acted as a reasonable person, along with the elements of negligence. The jury considers the defendant's conduct in relation to what the defendant knows or experienced.

For example, consider a defendant working on a loading dock and tossing large grain bags onto a truck. The defendant noticed two children playing near the truck. The defendant threw a bag towards the truck and unintentionally struck one child. A jury considers the defendant's knowledge that children were playing nearby when determining whether the defendant acted reasonably. The defendant would be liable for negligence if the defendant owed a duty to the child. The defendant's actual knowledge, a jury considers common knowledge. The defendant would be liable for knowing that a bag of grain could injure a child and the natural propensities of children for attractive nuisances.

Children

A child generally is not expected to act as a reasonable adult. Instead, courts hold children to a modified standard. Under this standard, a child's actions are compared with other children of the same age, experience, and intelligence. However, courts in some jurisdictions apply the adult standard of care to children who engage in certain adult activities (e.g., driving).

Direct and circumstantial evidence

Negligence is usually proven through direct evidence (e.g., witness's personal knowledge, images in a photograph, or video) or circumstantial evidence.

Circumstantial evidence requires a fact-finder to draw an inference based on the evidence.

Proving negligence by circumstances

Courts have rules governing proof in specific types of negligence. Negligence in a dog bite case is proven differently than in medical malpractice. In a slip-and-fall case, where a plaintiff's injury occurs due to a condition on the defendant's property, courts require the plaintiff to prove that the condition existed for such time that the defendant should have discovered and remedied the condition.

For example, a plaintiff who sues a supermarket when she slips on spilled liquid laundry soap could not recover from the supermarket without showing that the liquid had been on the floor long enough for the supermarket to have discovered it. Evidence that the soap was smeared across the floor due to the number of customers walking on the liquid may be sufficient proof.

Proving negligence with sparse evidence

A plaintiff, in some instances, may rely on the doctrine of *res ipsa loquitur* [Latin, *the thing speaks for itself*]. This legal theory allows a jury to infer that a defendant acted negligently, even without other proof. The plaintiff must prove that the event that occurred usually does not occur in the absence of negligence, and the defendant had exclusive control of the instrument causing the injury.

For example, a child injured by the bag of grain on a public sidewalk in front of a grain producer may not have any direct or circumstantial proof that the producer was negligent in handling the bag. However, a bag of grain typically does enter a public sidewalk in the absence of negligence. The producer presumably had exclusive control over the bag at the time of the accident. In this instance, the jury may infer negligence under *res ipsa loquitur*.

Notes for active learning

Causation

Causation in fact and proximate causation

A person who commits a negligent act is not liable unless this act was the cause of the plaintiff's injuries. Courts divided causation into two categories—causation in fact and proximate causation—and require each to be shown before the plaintiff may recover damages.

Causation in fact means that the defendant's negligence must be the actual cause of the plaintiff's injuries. For example, suppose a corporation negligently pollutes the drinking water. The plaintiff dies of a heart attack unrelated to the polluted water. Although the corporation has acted negligently, it is not liable for the plaintiff's death. Thus, there was no cause-and-effect relationship.

Causation in fact is "but for" causation, which means "but for the defendant's conduct, the plaintiff would not have suffered harm."

Proximate cause makes the defendant liable. It is a legal judgment call that concerns foreseeability. Based on public policy, the law establishes a point along the damage chain after which the negligent party is no longer responsible for the consequences of their actions. Beyond that point, there is no proximate cause. Proximate cause is examined on a case-by-case basis and could have been foreseen. It is extinguished by superseding (or *intervening*) causes.

Strict liability for product liability

The California Supreme Court (1963) first adopted the doctrine of strict liability in torts. The doctrine of strict liability removes many of the difficulties for the plaintiff associated with other theories of product liability. Strict liability can be traced to the Restatement (Second) of Torts, which provides that one who sells any product in a defective condition unreasonably dangerous to the user is subject to liability for physical harm caused to the consumer.

Strict liability is applied even though the defendant has exercised all possible care in the preparation and sale of the product and even though the user or consumer has not bought the product from the seller. Strict liability applies only to products and not services and applies to those who are in the business of selling or leasing products. All parties in the "chain of distribution" of a defective product are strictly liable for the injuries caused by that product.

Thus, all manufacturers, distributors, wholesalers, retailers, lessors, and subcomponent manufacturers may be sued under this doctrine. A defendant who has not been negligent but made to pay a strict liability judgment can then bring a separate action against the negligent party in the chain of distribution to recover its losses. Those parties who can recover under strict liability include the purchaser or lessee, family members, guests, employees, customers, and persons who passively enjoy the benefits of the product (for example, passengers in automobiles).

The damages recoverable in a strict liability action vary by jurisdiction, but personal injury damages are recoverable everywhere. Property damage is recoverable in most jurisdictions, and economic loss is recoverable in just a few jurisdictions. Punitive damages can also be recovered in a strict liability action.

Defamation

Libel, slander and defamation

There is an intricate balance between one person's right to freedom of speech and another's right to protect their good name. It is often difficult to know which personal remarks are proper and which are defamatory.

Defamation (or *deformation of character*) is an all-encompassing term covering statements that hurt someone's reputation. Defamation includes:

> *Libel* – a statement written and seen by another.

> *Slander* – the statement spoken and heard by another.

Defamation is considered to be a civil wrong (or *tort*). A person who has suffered a defamatory statement may sue the person who made the statement under the tort of defamation.

Defamation law balances freedom of speech and the right to avoid harm to reputation. A reasonable person should have free speech to talk truthfully without fear of a lawsuit if they say something unflattering but true.

Conversely, people have a right not to have false statements damage their reputations. Determining a statement of fact is an *absolute defense* once proven. The prevailing side may sue for damages.

Elements for defamation

Defamation is governed by state law, but some standards apply. Generally, the plaintiff must prove:

1. Someone made a statement;

2. The statement was published;

3. The statement caused the plaintiff injury;

4. The statement was false; and

5. The statement was not privileged.

Elements defined

Statement - A "statement" needs to be spoken (slander), written (libel), or otherwise expressed. Because spoken words often fade quickly from memory, slander is considered less harmful than libel. These statements are especially damaging if they involve sexual misconduct, character dispersions, or the abuse of minors.

Publication – For a statement to be published, a third party (someone other than the person making or the subject of the statement) must have seen, heard, or read the defamatory statement. Unlike the traditional meaning of "published," the defamatory statement does not need to be printed. Instead, a statement heard over the television or seen scrawled on the bathroom wall is published.

Injury - The statement must be shown to have injured the person by hurting their reputation. For example, a statement caused injury if the subject of the statement lost work as a result of the statement.

Falsity - Defamation law only considers statements actionable if they are false. A true statement is not considered defamation. Additionally, statements of opinion are not considered false because they are subjective to the speaker.

Unprivileged - For a statement to be defamatory, it must not be privileged. A person is not liable for defamation if the statement is privileged. For example, if a witness testifies at trial and makes false and injurious statements, the witness is immune to defamation because testimony at trial is privileged.

Social media and defamation

It is easy to make a defamatory statement with social media by publishing a statement reaching millions instantly. Whether it is a disparaging blog post, status update, or video, online defamation is treated like traditional forms; the user can be held liable for defamatory statements posted online.

Public officials and figures require malice

There is a high priority on the public being allowed to speak about elected officials and public figures. Elected and public figures get less protection from defamatory statements and face a higher burden when attempting to prove and prevail in a defamation lawsuit.

When an official is criticized in a false and injurious way related to their behavior in office, the official must prove the elements of typical defamation and show that the statement was made with "actual malice."

Actual malice was defined in *Hustler v. Falwell* (1988) when the Supreme Court held that the First Amendment freedom of speech protected certain statements that would otherwise be defamatory.

Public officials only prevail in a defamation suit when the statement was not an honest mistake and was published with the intent to harm. Actual malice only occurs when the person making the statement knew the statement was not true or had a *reckless disregard* for whether it was true.

Overview of American Law

Overview of American Law

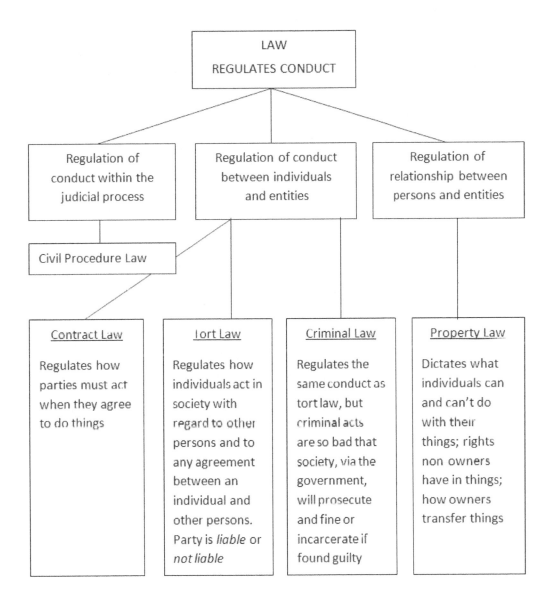

U.S. Court Systems – Federal and State Courts

There are two kinds of courts in the USA – federal courts and state courts.

Federal courts are established under the U.S. Constitution by Congress to decide disputes involving the Constitution and laws passed by Congress. A state establishes state and local courts (within states, local courts are established by cities, counties, and other municipalities).

Jurisdiction of federal and state courts

The differences between federal courts and state courts are defined by jurisdiction.[1] Jurisdiction refers to the kinds of cases that a particular court is authorized to hear and adjudicate (i.e., the pronouncement of a legally binding judgment upon the parties to the dispute).

Federal court jurisdiction is limited to the types of cases listed in the Constitution and specifically provided by Congress. For the most part, federal courts only hear:

- cases in which the United States is a party[2];

- cases involving violations of the U.S. Constitution or federal laws (under federal-question jurisdiction[3]);

- cases between citizens of different states if the amount in controversy *exceeds* $75,000 (under diversity jurisdiction[4]); and

- bankruptcy, copyright, patent, and maritime law cases.

State courts, in contrast, have broad jurisdiction, so the cases individual citizens are likely to be involved in (e.g., robberies, traffic violations, contracts, and family disputes) are usually heard and decided in state courts. The only cases state courts are not allowed to hear are lawsuits against the United States and those involving certain specific federal laws: criminal, antitrust, bankruptcy, patent, copyright, and some maritime law cases.

In many cases, both federal and state courts have jurisdiction whereby the plaintiff (i.e., the party initiating the suit) can choose whether to file their claim in state or federal court.

Criminal cases involving federal laws can be tried only in federal court, but most criminal cases involve violations of state law and are tried in state court. Robbery is a crime, but what law makes it is a crime? Except for certain exceptions, state laws, not federal laws, make robbery a crime. There are only a few federal laws about robbery, such as the law that makes it a federal crime to rob a bank whose deposits are insured by a federal agency. Examples of other federal crimes are the transport of illegal drugs into the country or across state lines and using the U.S. mail system to defraud consumers.

Crimes committed on federal property (e.g., national parks or military reservations) are prosecuted in federal court.

Federal courts may hear cases concerning state laws if the issue is whether the state law violates the federal Constitution. Suppose a state law forbids slaughtering animals outside of certain limited areas. A neighborhood association brings a case in state court against a defendant who sacrifices chickens in their backyard. When the court issues an order (i.e., an injunction[5]) forbidding the defendant from further sacrifices, the defendant challenges the state law in federal court as an unconstitutional infringement of religious freedom.

Some conduct is illegal under both federal and state laws. For example, federal laws prohibit employment discrimination, and the states have added additional legal restrictions. A person can file their claim in either federal or state court under federal law or federal and state laws. A case that only involves a state law can be brought only in state court.

Appeals for review of actions by federal administrative agencies are federal civil cases.

For example, if the Environmental Protection Agency, over the objection of area residents, issued a permit to a paper mill to discharge water used in its milling process into the Scenic River, the residents may appeal and have the federal court of appeals review the agency's decision.

[1] *jurisdiction* – 1) the legal authority of a court to hear and decide specific types of case; 2) the geographic area over which the court has the authority to decide cases.

[2] *parties* – the plaintiff and the defendant in a lawsuit.

[3] *federal-question jurisdiction* – the federal district courts' authorization to hear and decide cases arising under the Constitution, laws, or treaties of the United States.

[4] *diversity jurisdiction* – the federal district courts' authority to hear and decide civil cases involving plaintiffs and defendants who are citizens of different states (or U.S. citizens and foreign nationals) and meet specific statutory requirements.

[5] *injunction* – a judge's order that a party takes or refrain from taking a particular action. An injunction may be preliminary until the outcome of a case is determined or permanent.

Organization of the federal courts

Congress has divided the country into 94 federal judicial districts, with each having a U.S. district court. The U.S. district courts are the federal trial courts -- where federal cases are tried, witnesses testify, and juries serve.

Each district has a U.S. bankruptcy court, which is part of the district court that administers the U.S. bankruptcy laws.

Congress uses state boundaries to help define the districts. Some districts cover an entire state, like Idaho. Other districts cover just part of a state, like the Northern District of California. Congress placed each of the ninety-four districts in one of twelve regional circuits whereby each circuit has a court of appeals. The losing party can petition the court of appeals to review the case to determine if the district judge applied the law correctly.

There is a U.S. Court of Appeals for the Federal Circuit, whose jurisdiction is defined by subject matter rather than geography. It hears appeals from certain courts and agencies, such as the U.S. Court of International Trade, the U.S. Court of Federal Claims, and the U.S. Patent and Trademark Office, and certain types of cases from the district courts (mainly lawsuits claiming that patents have been infringed).

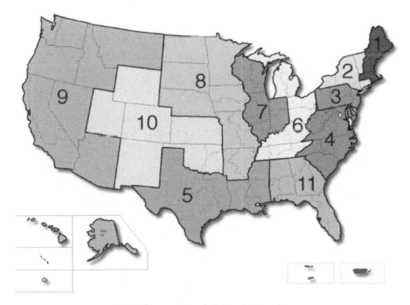

Twelve regional federal circuits

The Supreme Court in Washington, D.C., is the highest court in the nation. The losing party can petition in a case in the court of appeals (or, sometimes, in a state supreme court), can petition the Supreme Court to hear an appeal.

Unlike a court of appeals, the Supreme Court does not have to hear the case. The Supreme Court hears only a small percentage of the cases it is asked to review.

Notes for active learning

How Civil Cases Move Through the Federal Courts

A federal civil case begins when a person, or their legal representative, files a paper with the clerk of the court that asserts another person's wrongful act injured the person. In legal terminology, the plaintiff files a *complaint* against the defendant.

The defendant files an *answer* to the complaint. These written statements of the party's positions are called pleadings. In some circumstances, the defendant may file a *motion* instead of an answer; the motion asks the court to take some action, such as dismiss the case or require the plaintiff to explain more clearly what the lawsuit is about.

Jury trials

In a jury trial, the jury decides what happened, and to apply the legal standards, the judge tells them to apply to reach a verdict The plaintiff presents evidence supporting its view of the case, and the defendant presents evidence rebutting the plaintiff's evidence or supporting its view of the case. From these presentations, the jury must decide what happened and applied the law to those facts.

The jury never decides what law applies to the case; that is the role of the judge. For example, in a discrimination case where the plaintiff alleged that their workplace was hostile, the judge tells the jury the legal standard for a hostile environment.

The jury would have to decide whether the plaintiff's description of events was true and whether those events met the legal standard. A trial jury, or petit jury, may consist of six to twelve jurors in a civil case.

Bench trials

If the parties agree not to have a *jury trial* and leave the fact-finding to the judge, the trial is a *bench trial*. In bench and jury trials, the judge ensures the correct legal standards are followed.

In contrast to a jury trial, the judge decides the facts and renders the verdict in a *bench trial*.

For example, in a discrimination case in which the plaintiff alleged a hostile environment, the judge would determine the legal standard for a hostile environment and decide whether the plaintiff's description of events was true and whether those events met the legal standard.

Some kinds of cases always have bench trials. For example, there is never a jury trial if the plaintiff is seeking an injunction, an order from the judge that the defendant does, or stop doing something, as opposed to monetary damages.

Some statutes provide that a judge must decide the facts in certain types of cases.

Jury selection

A jury trial begins with the selection of jurors. Citizens are selected for jury service through a process set out in laws passed by Congress and in the federal rules of procedure.

First, citizens are called to court to be available to serve on juries. These citizens are selected at random from sources, in most districts, lists of registered voters, which may be augmented by other sources, such as lists of licensed drivers in the judicial district.

The judge and the lawyers choose who will serve on the jury.

To choose the jurors, the judge and sometimes the lawyers ask prospective jurors questions to determine if they will decide the case fairly, a process known as *voir dire*.

The lawyers may request that the judge excuse jurors they think may not be impartial, such as those who know a party in the case or who have had an experience that might make them favor one side over the other. These requests for rejecting jurors are *challenges for cause*.

The lawyers may request that the judge excuse a certain number of jurors without reason; these requests are *peremptory challenges*.

Instructions and standard of proof

Following the closing arguments, the judge gives instructions to the jury, explaining the relevant law, how the law applies to the case, and what questions the jury must decide.

How sure do jurors have to be before they reach a verdict? One important instruction the judge gives the jury is the standard of proof they must follow in deciding the case.

The courts, through their decisions, and Congress, through statutes, have established standards by which facts must be proven in criminal and civil cases.

In civil cases, to decide for the plaintiff, the jury must determine by a *preponderance of the evidence* that the defendant failed to perform a legal duty and violated the plaintiff's rights. A preponderance of the evidence means that, based on the evidence, the evidence favors the plaintiff more (even if only slightly) than it favors the defendant.

If the evidence in favor of the plaintiff could be placed on one side of a scale and that in favor of the defendant on the other, the plaintiff would win if the evidence in favor of the plaintiff was heavy enough to tip the scale. If the two sides were even, or if the scale tipped for the defendant, the defendant would win.

Judgment

In civil cases, if the jury (or judge) decides in favor of the plaintiff, the result usually is that the defendant must pay the plaintiff money or damages. The judge orders the defendant to pay the decided amount. Sometimes the defendant is ordered to take some specific action that will restore the plaintiff's rights. If the defendant wins the case, there is nothing more the trial court needs to do as the case is disposed of and the defendant is held not liable.

Right to appeal

The losing party in a federal civil case has a right to appeal the verdict to the U.S. court of appeals (i.e., Federal Circuit Courts) and ask the court to review the case to determine whether the trial was conducted properly. The losing party in the state trial court has a right to appeal the verdict to the state court of appeal.

The grounds for appeal usually are that the federal district (or state) judge made an error, either in the procedure (e.g., admitting improper evidence) or interpreting the law. The government may appeal in civil cases, as any other party may. Neither party may appeal if there was no trial -- parties settled their civil case out of court.

Notes for active learning

How Criminal Cases Move Through the Federal Courts

Indictment or information

A criminal case formally begins with an indictment or information, which is a formal accusation that a person committed a crime.

An indictment may be obtained when a lawyer (i.e., prosecutor) for the executive branch of the U.S. government (i.e., U.S. attorney or assistant U.S. attorney) present evidence to a federal grand jury that, according to the government, indicates a person committed a crime.

The U.S. attorney tries to convince the grand jury that there is enough evidence to show that the person probably committed the crime and should be formally accused. If the grand jury agrees, it issues an indictment.

A grand jury is different from a trial jury or petit jury.

A grand jury determines whether the person may be tried for a crime; a petit jury listens to the evidence presented at the trial and determines whether the defendant is guilty.

Petit is French for "small"; petit juries usually consist of twelve jurors in criminal cases.

Grand is French for "large"; grand juries have from sixteen to twenty-three jurors.

Grand jury indictments are most often used for *felonies* (i.e., punishable by imprisonment of more than a year or by death) such as bank robberies or sales of illegal drugs.

Grand jury indictments are not necessary to prosecute *misdemeanors* (i.e., less serious than a felony but more serious than an infraction) and are necessary for felonies.

For lesser crimes, the U.S. attorney issues an *information* that substitutes for an indictment. For example, speeding on a highway in a national park is a misdemeanor.

An information is used when a defendant waives an indictment by a grand jury.

Arraignment

After the grand jury issues the indictment, the accused (i.e., defendant) is summoned to court or arrested (if not already in custody). The next step is an arraignment, a proceeding in which the defendant is brought before a judge, told of the charges they are accused of, and asked to plead guilty or not guilty. If the defendant's plea is guilty, a time is set for the defendant to return to court to be sentenced.

If the defendant pleads "not guilty," the time is set for the trial.

A defendant may enter a plea bargain with the prosecution--usually by agreeing to plead guilty to some but not all charges or lesser charges. The prosecution drops the remaining charges.

About nine out of ten defendants in criminal cases plead guilty.

Investigation

In a criminal case, a defense lawyer conducts a thorough investigation before trial, interviewing witnesses, visiting the crime scene, and examining physical evidence. An important part of this investigation is determining whether the evidence the government plans to use to prove its case was obtained legally.

The Fourth Amendment to the Constitution forbids unreasonable searches and seizures. To enforce this protection, the Supreme Court has decided that illegally seized evidence cannot be used at trial for most purposes.

For example, if the police seize evidence from a defendant's home without a search warrant, the lawyer for the defendant can ask the court to exclude the evidence from use at trial. The court holds a hearing to determine whether the search was unreasonable.

If the court rules that key evidence was seized illegally and cannot be used, the government often drops the charges against the defendant.

If the government has a strong case and the court ruled that the evidence was obtained legally, the defendant may decide to plead guilty rather than go to trial, where a conviction is likely.

Deliberations and verdict

After receiving its instructions from the judge, the jury retires to the jury room to discuss the evidence and reach a verdict (a decision on the factual issues). A criminal jury verdict must be unanimous; all jurors must agree that the defendant is guilty or not guilty.

If the jurors cannot agree, the judge declares a mistrial, and the prosecutor must decide whether to ask the court to dismiss the case or have it presented to another jury.

Judgment and sentencing

In federal criminal cases, if the jury (or judge, if there is no jury) decides that the defendant is guilty, the judge sets a date for a sentencing hearing. In federal criminal cases, the jury does not decide whether the defendant will go to prison or for how long; the judge does.

In federal death penalty cases, the jury does decide whether the defendant will receive a death sentence. Sentencing statutes passed by Congress control the judge's sentencing decision. Additionally, judges use Sentencing Guidelines, issued by the U.S. Sentencing Commission, as a source of advice as to the proper sentence. The guidelines consider the nature of the offense and the offender's criminal history.

A presentence report, prepared by one of the court's probation officers, provides the judge with information about the offender and the offense, including the sentence recommended by the guidelines. After determining the sentence, the judge signs a judgment, including the plea, the verdict, and sentence.

Right to appeal

A defendant who is found guilty in a federal criminal trial has a right to appeal the decision to the U.S. court of appeals, that is, ask the court of appeals to review the case to determine whether the trial was conducted properly. The grounds for appeal are usually that the district judge is said to have made an error, either in a procedure (admitting improper evidence, for example) or interpreting the law.

A defendant who pled guilty may not appeal the conviction.

A defendant who pled guilty may have the right to appeal their sentence.

The government may not appeal if a defendant in a criminal case is found not guilty because the Double Jeopardy Clause of the Fifth Amendment to the Constitution provides that no person shall "be twice put in jeopardy of life or limb" for the same offense.

This reflects society's belief that, even if a subsequent trial might finally find a defendant guilty, it is not proper for the government to harass an acquitted defendant through repeated retrials.

However, the government may sometimes appeal a sentence.

Notes for active learning

How Civil and Criminal Appeals Move Through the Federal Courts

Assignment of Judges

Alternative Dispute Resolution (ADR)

Review of Lower Court Decision

Oral Argument

Decision

The Supreme Court of the United States

Assignment of judges

The courts of appeals usually assign cases to a panel of three judges. The panel decides the case for the entire court. Sometimes, when the parties request it or a question of unusual importance, the judges on the appeals court assemble *en banc* (a rare event).

Review of a lower court decision

In making its decision, the panel reviews key parts of the record. The record consists of the documents filed in the case at trial and the transcript of the trial proceedings. The panel learns about the lawyers' legal arguments from the lawyers' briefs.

Briefs are written documents that each side submits to explain its case and tell why the court should decide in its favor.

Oral argument

If the court permits oral argument, the lawyers for each side have a limited amount of time (typically between 15 to 30 minutes) to argue (i.e., advocate and explain) their case to the judges (or justices at the highest court in the jurisdiction) in a formal courtroom session. The judges (or justices for the highest court in the jurisdiction) frequently question the attorneys about the relevant law as it applies to the facts and issues in the case before them.

A court of appeals differs from the federal trial courts. There are no jurors, witnesses, or court reporters. The lawyers for each side, but not the parties, are usually present in the courtroom.

Decision

After the submission of briefs and oral arguments, the judges discuss the case privately, consider relevant *precedents* (court decisions from higher courts in prior cases with similar facts and legal issues), and reach a decision. Courts are required to follow precedents.

For example, a U.S. court of appeals must follow the U.S. Supreme Court's decisions; a district court must follow the decisions of the U.S. Supreme Court and the decisions of the court of appeals of its circuit.

Courts are influenced by decisions they are not required to follow, such as the decisions of other circuits. Courts follow precedent unless they set forth reasons for the diversion.

At least two of the three judges on the panel must agree on a decision. One judge who agrees with the decision is chosen to write an opinion, which announces and explains the decision.

If a judge on the panel disagrees with the majority's opinion, the judge may write a dissent, giving reasons for disagreeing.

Many appellate opinions are published in books of opinions, called reporters. The opinions are read carefully by other judges and lawyers looking for precedents to guide them in their cases.

The accumulated judicial opinions make up a body of law known as *case law*, which is usually an accurate predictor of how future cases will be decided.

For decisions that the judges believe are important to the parties and contribute little to the law, the appeals courts frequently use short, unsigned opinions that often are not published.

If the court of appeals decides that the trial judge incorrectly interpreted the law or followed incorrect procedures, it reverses the district court's decision.

For example, the court of appeals could hold that the district judge allowed the jury to base its decision on evidence that never should have been admitted, and thus the defendant cannot be guilty.

Most of the time, courts of appeals uphold, rather than the reverse, district court decisions.

Sometimes when a higher court reverses the decision of the district court, it sends the case back (i.e., *remand* the case) to the lower court for another trial.

For example, *Miranda v. Arizona* case (1966), the Supreme Court ruled 5-4 that Ernesto Miranda's confession could not be used as evidence because he had not been advised of his right to remain silent or of his right to have a lawyer present during questioning.

However, the government did have other evidence against him. The case was remanded for a new trial, in which the improperly obtained confession was not used as evidence, but the other evidence convicted Miranda.

The Supreme Court of the United States

The Supreme Court is the highest in the nation. It is a different kind of appeals court; its major function is not correcting errors made by trial judges but clarifying the law in cases of national importance or when lower courts disagree about interpreting the Constitution or federal laws.

The Supreme Court does not have to hear every case that it is asked to review. Each year, losing parties ask the Supreme Court to review about 8,000 cases.

Almost all cases come to the Court as a *petition for writ of certiorari*. The court selects only about 80 to 120 of the most significant cases to review with oral arguments.

Supreme Court decisions establish a precedent for interpreting the Constitution and federal laws; holdings that state and federal courts must follow.

The power of judicial review makes the Supreme Court's role in our government vital. Judicial review is the power of a court when deciding a case to declare that a law passed by a legislature or action by the executive branch is invalid because it is inconsistent with the Constitution.

Although district courts, courts of appeals, and state courts can exercise the power of judicial review, their decisions about federal law are always subject, on appeal, to review by the Supreme Court.

When the Supreme Court declares a law unconstitutional, its decision can only be overruled by a later decision of the Supreme Court or Amendment to the Constitution.

Seven of the twenty-seven Amendments to the Constitution have invalidated the decisions of the Supreme Court. However, most Supreme Court cases do not concern the constitutionality of laws, but the interpretation of laws passed by Congress.

Although Congress has steadily increased the number of district and appeals court judges over the years, the Supreme Court has remained the same size since 1869. It consists of a Chief Justice and eight associate justices.

Like the federal court of appeals and federal district judges, the Supreme Court justices are appointed by the President with the Senate's *advice and consent*.

Unlike the judges in the courts of appeals, Supreme Court justices never sit on panels. Absent recusal, nine justices hear cases, and a majority ruling decides cases.

The Supreme Court begins its annual session, or term, on the first Monday of October. The term lasts until the Court has announced its decisions in cases where it has heard an argument that term—usually late June or early July.

During the term, the Court, sitting for two weeks at a time, hears oral arguments on Monday through Wednesday and holds private conferences to discuss the cases, reach decisions, and begin preparing the written opinions that explain its decisions.

Most decisions and opinions are released in the late spring and early summer.

Standards of review for federal courts

Standard of review	De novo	Clearly erroneous	Abuse of discretion
Type of decision under review	Question of the law	Question of fact	Discretionary action
Lower-court decision maker	Trial judge	Trial judge	Trial judge
Deference given to lower court	No deference	Substantial deference	Extreme deference
Party typically benefitted	Appellant	Appellee	Appellee
Definition	An appellate court reviews the legal question anew and independently, without regard to the conclusions reached by the trial court. "When *de novo* review is compelled, no form of appellate deference is acceptable." *Salve Regina College v. Russell*, (1991).	A finding is 'clearly erroneous' when although there is evidence to support it, the reviewing court on the entire evidence is left with the definite and firm conviction that a mistake has been committed. *United States v. United States Gypsum Co.*, (1948) "If the district court's account of the evidence is plausible in light of the record viewed in its entirety, the court of appeals may not reverse it even though convinced that had it been sitting as the trier of fact, it would have weighed the evidence differently. When there are two permissible views of the evidence, the factfinder's choice between them cannot be clearly erroneous." *Anderson v. Bessemer City*, (1985).	Generally, an abuse of discretion only occurs where no reasonable person could take the view adopted by the trial court. If reasonable persons could differ, no abuse of discretion can be found. *Harrington v. DeVito*, (7th Cir.1981) Under the abuse of discretion standard, a trial court's decision will not be disturbed unless the appellate court has a definite and firm conviction that the lower court made a clear error of judgment or exceeded the bounds of permissible choice in the circumstances. We will not alter a trial court's decision unless it can be shown that the court's decision was an arbitrary, capricious, whimsical, or manifestly unreasonable judgment. *Wright v. Abbott Laboratories, Inc.*, (10th Cir. 2001)
Examples	Motions for summary judgment, constitutional questions, statutory interpretation	Questions regarding who did what, where, and when; questions of intent and motive; questions of ultimate fact (such as negligence)	Rule 11 sanctions, attorney's fees, courtroom management, motions to compel, injunctions, and temporary restraining orders.

The Constitution of the United States (*a transcription*)

THE U.S. NATIONAL ARCHIVES & RECORDS ADMINISTRATION
www.archives.gov

The following text is a transcription of the Constitution as it was inscribed by Jacob Shallus on parchment (the document on display in the Rotunda at the National Archives Museum.) The spelling and punctuation reflect the original.

The Constitution of the United States: A Transcription

The following text is a transcription of the Constitution as it was inscribed by Jacob Shallus on parchment (displayed in the Rotunda at the National Archives Museum.) The authenticated text of the Constitution can be found on the website of the Government Printing Office.

We the People of the United States, in Order to form a more perfect Union, establish Justice, insure domestic Tranquility, provide for the common defence, promote the general Welfare, and secure the Blessings of Liberty to ourselves and our Posterity, do ordain and establish this Constitution for the United States of America.

Article. I

Section. 1.

All legislative Powers herein granted shall be vested in a Congress of the United States, which shall consist of a Senate and House of Representatives.

Section. 2.

The House of Representatives shall be composed of Members chosen every second Year by the People of the several States, and the Electors in each State shall have the Qualifications requisite for Electors of the most numerous Branch of the State Legislature.

No Person shall be a Representative who shall not have attained to the Age of twenty five Years, and been seven Years a Citizen of the United States, and who shall not, when elected, be an Inhabitant of that State in which he shall be chosen.

Representatives and direct Taxes shall be apportioned among the several States which may be included within this Union, according to their respective Numbers, which shall be determined by adding to the whole Number of free Persons, including those bound to Service for a Term of Years, and excluding Indians not taxed, three fifths of all other Persons. The actual Enumeration shall be made within three Years after the first Meeting of the Congress of the United States, and within every subsequent Term of ten Years, in such Manner as they shall by Law direct. The Number of Representatives shall not exceed one for every thirty Thousand, but each State shall have at Least one Representative; and until such enumeration shall be made, the State of New Hampshire shall be entitled to chuse three, Massachusetts eight, Rhode-Island and Providence

Plantations one, Connecticut five, New-York six, New Jersey four, Pennsylvania eight, Delaware one, Maryland six, Virginia ten, North Carolina five, South Carolina five, and Georgia three.

When vacancies happen in the Representation from any State, the Executive Authority thereof shall issue Writs of Election to fill such Vacancies.

The House of Representatives shall chuse their Speaker and other Officers; and shall have the sole Power of Impeachment.

Section. 3.

The Senate of the United States shall be composed of two Senators from each State, chosen by the Legislature thereof, for six Years; and each Senator shall have one Vote.

Immediately after they shall be assembled in Consequence of the first Election, they shall be divided as equally as may be into three Classes. The Seats of the Senators of the first Class shall be vacated at the Expiration of the second Year, of the second Class at the Expiration of the fourth Year, and of the third Class at the Expiration of the sixth Year, so that one third may be chosen every second Year; and if Vacancies happen by Resignation, or otherwise, during the Recess of the Legislature of any State, the Executive thereof may make temporary Appointments until the next Meeting of the Legislature, which shall then fill such Vacancies.

No Person shall be a Senator who shall not have attained to the Age of thirty Years, and been nine Years a Citizen of the United States, and who shall not, when elected, be an Inhabitant of that State for which he shall be chosen.

The Vice President of the United States shall be President of the Senate, but shall have no Vote, unless they be equally divided.

The Senate shall chuse their other Officers, and also a President pro tempore, in the Absence of the Vice President, or when he shall exercise the Office of President of the United States.

The Senate shall have the sole Power to try all Impeachments. When sitting for that Purpose, they shall be on Oath or Affirmation. When the President of the United States is tried, the Chief Justice shall preside: And no Person shall be convicted without the Concurrence of two thirds of the Members present.

Judgment in Cases of Impeachment shall not extend further than to removal from Office, and disqualification to hold and enjoy any Office of honor, Trust or Profit under the United States: but the Party convicted shall nevertheless be liable and subject to Indictment, Trial, Judgment and Punishment, according to Law.

Section. 4.

The Times, Places and Manner of holding Elections for Senators and Representatives, shall be prescribed in each State by the Legislature thereof; but the Congress may at any time by Law make or alter such Regulations, except as to the Places of chusing Senators.

The Congress shall assemble at least once in every Year, and such Meeting shall be on the first Monday in December, unless they shall by Law appoint a different Day.

Section. 5.

Each House shall be the Judge of the Elections, Returns and Qualifications of its own Members, and a Majority of each shall constitute a Quorum to do Business; but a smaller Number may adjourn from day to day, and may be authorized to compel the Attendance of absent Members, in such Manner, and under such Penalties as each House may provide.

Each House may determine the Rules of its Proceedings, punish its Members for disorderly Behaviour, and, with the Concurrence of two thirds, expel a Member.

Each House shall keep a Journal of its Proceedings, and from time to time publish the same, excepting such Parts as may in their Judgment require Secrecy; and the Yeas and Nays of the Members of either House on any question shall, at the Desire of one fifth of those Present, be entered on the Journal.

Neither House, during the Session of Congress, shall, without the Consent of the other, adjourn for more than three days, nor to any other Place than that in which the two Houses shall be sitting.

Section. 6.

The Senators and Representatives shall receive a Compensation for their Services, to be ascertained by Law, and paid out of the Treasury of the United States. They shall in all Cases, except Treason, Felony and Breach of the Peace, be privileged from Arrest during their Attendance at the Session of their respective Houses, and in going to and returning from the same; and for any Speech or Debate in either House, they shall not be questioned in any other Place.

No Senator or Representative shall, during the Time for which he was elected, be appointed to any civil Office under the Authority of the United States, which shall have been created, or the Emoluments whereof shall have been encreased during such time; and no Person holding any Office under the United States, shall be a Member of either House during his Continuance in Office.

Section. 7.

All Bills for raising Revenue shall originate in the House of Representatives; but the Senate may propose or concur with Amendments as on other Bills.

Every Bill which shall have passed the House of Representatives and the Senate, shall, before it become a Law, be presented to the President of the United States; If he approves he shall sign it, but if not he shall return it, with his Objections to that House in which it shall have originated, who shall enter the Objections at large on their Journal, and proceed to reconsider it. If after such Reconsideration two thirds of that House shall agree to pass the Bill, it shall be sent, together with the Objections, to the other House, by which it shall likewise be reconsidered, and if approved by two thirds of that House, it shall become a Law. But in all such Cases the Votes of both Houses shall be determined by yeas and Nays, and the Names of the Persons voting for and against the Bill shall be entered on the Journal of each House respectively. If any Bill shall not be returned by the President within ten Days (Sundays excepted) after it shall have been presented to him, the Same shall be a Law, in like Manner as if he had signed it, unless the Congress by their Adjournment prevent its Return, in which Case it shall not be a Law.

Every Order, Resolution, or Vote to which the Concurrence of the Senate and House of Representatives may be necessary (except on a question of Adjournment) shall be presented to the President of the United States; and before the Same shall take Effect, shall be approved by him, or being disapproved by him, shall be repassed by two thirds of the Senate and House of Representatives, according to the Rules and Limitations prescribed in the Case of a Bill.

Section. 8.

The Congress shall have Power To lay and collect Taxes, Duties, Imposts and Excises, to pay the Debts and provide for the common Defence and general Welfare of the United States; but all Duties, Imposts and Excises shall be uniform throughout the United States;

To borrow Money on the credit of the United States;

To regulate Commerce with foreign Nations, and among the several States, and with the Indian Tribes;

To establish an uniform Rule of Naturalization, and uniform Laws on the subject of Bankruptcies throughout the United States;

To coin Money, regulate the Value thereof, and of foreign Coin, and fix the Standard of Weights and Measures;

To provide for the Punishment of counterfeiting the Securities and current Coin of the United States;

To establish Post Offices and post Roads;

To promote the Progress of Science and useful Arts, by securing for limited Times to Authors and Inventors the exclusive Right to their respective Writings and Discoveries;

To constitute Tribunals inferior to the Supreme Court;

To define and punish Piracies and Felonies committed on the high Seas, and Offences against the Law of Nations;

To declare War, grant Letters of Marque and Reprisal, and make Rules concerning Captures on Land and Water;

To raise and support Armies, but no Appropriation of Money to that Use shall be for a longer Term than two Years;

To provide and maintain a Navy;

To make Rules for the Government and Regulation of the land and naval Forces;

To provide for calling forth the Militia to execute the Laws of the Union, suppress Insurrections and repel Invasions;

To provide for organizing, arming, and disciplining, the Militia, and for governing such Part of them as may be employed in the Service of the United States, reserving to the States respectively, the Appointment of the Officers, and the Authority of training the Militia according to the discipline prescribed by Congress;

To exercise exclusive Legislation in all Cases whatsoever, over such District (not exceeding ten Miles square) as may, by Cession of particular States, and the Acceptance of Congress, become the Seat of the Government of the United States, and to exercise like Authority over all Places purchased by the Consent of the Legislature of the State in which the Same shall be, for the Erection of Forts, Magazines, Arsenals, dock-Yards, and other needful Buildings;—And

To make all Laws which shall be necessary and proper for carrying into Execution the foregoing Powers, and all other Powers vested by this Constitution in the Government of the United States, or in any Department or Officer thereof.

Section. 9.

The Migration or Importation of such Persons as any of the States now existing shall think proper to admit, shall not be prohibited by the Congress prior to the Year one thousand eight hundred and eight, but a Tax or duty may be imposed on such Importation, not exceeding ten dollars for each Person.

The Privilege of the Writ of Habeas Corpus shall not be suspended, unless when in Cases of Rebellion or Invasion the public Safety may require it.

No Bill of Attainder or ex post facto Law shall be passed.

No Capitation, or other direct, Tax shall be laid, unless in Proportion to the Census or enumeration herein before directed to be taken.

No Tax or Duty shall be laid on Articles exported from any State.

No Preference shall be given by any Regulation of Commerce or Revenue to the Ports of one State over those of another: nor shall Vessels bound to, or from, one State, be obliged to enter, clear, or pay Duties in another.

No Money shall be drawn from the Treasury, but in Consequence of Appropriations made by Law; and a regular Statement and Account of the Receipts and Expenditures of all public Money shall be published from time to time.

No Title of Nobility shall be granted by the United States: And no Person holding any Office of Profit or Trust under them, shall, without the Consent of the Congress, accept of any present, Emolument, Office, or Title, of any kind whatever, from any King, Prince, or foreign State.

Section. 10.

No State shall enter into any Treaty, Alliance, or Confederation; grant Letters of Marque and Reprisal; coin Money; emit Bills of Credit; make any Thing but gold and silver Coin a Tender in Payment of Debts; pass any Bill of Attainder, ex post facto Law, or Law impairing the Obligation of Contracts, or grant any Title of Nobility.

No State shall, without the Consent of the Congress, lay any Imposts or Duties on Imports or Exports, except what may be absolutely necessary for executing it's inspection Laws: and the net

Produce of all Duties and Imposts, laid by any State on Imports or Exports, shall be for the Use of the Treasury of the United States; and all such Laws shall be subject to the Revision and Controul of the Congress.

No State shall, without the Consent of Congress, lay any Duty of Tonnage, keep Troops, or Ships of War in time of Peace, enter into any Agreement or Compact with another State, or with a foreign Power, or engage in War, unless actually invaded, or in such imminent Danger as will not admit of delay.

Article. II

Section. 1.

The executive Power shall be vested in a President of the United States of America. He shall hold his Office during the Term of four Years, and, together with the Vice President, chosen for the same Term, be elected, as follows

Each State shall appoint, in such Manner as the Legislature thereof may direct, a Number of Electors, equal to the whole Number of Senators and Representatives to which the State may be entitled in the Congress: but no Senator or Representative, or Person holding an Office of Trust or Profit under the United States, shall be appointed an Elector.

The Electors shall meet in their respective States, and vote by Ballot for two Persons, of whom one at least shall not be an Inhabitant of the same State with themselves. And they shall make a List of all the Persons voted for, and of the Number of Votes for each; which List they shall sign and certify, and transmit sealed to the Seat of the Government of the United States, directed to the President of the Senate. The President of the Senate shall, in the Presence of the Senate and House of Representatives, open all the Certificates, and the Votes shall then be counted. The Person having the greatest Number of Votes shall be the President, if such Number be a Majority of the whole Number of Electors appointed; and if there be more than one who have such Majority, and have an equal Number of Votes, then the House of Representatives shall immediately chuse by Ballot one of them for President; and if no Person have a Majority, then from the five highest on the List the said House shall in like Manner chuse the President. But in chusing the President, the Votes shall be taken by States, the Representation from each State having one Vote; A quorum for this Purpose shall consist of a Member or Members from two thirds of the States, and a Majority of all the States shall be necessary to a Choice. In every Case, after the Choice of the President, the Person having the greatest Number of Votes of the Electors shall be the Vice President. But if there should remain two or more who have equal Votes, the Senate shall chuse from them by Ballot the Vice President.

The Congress may determine the Time of chusing the Electors, and the Day on which they shall give their Votes; which Day shall be the same throughout the United States.

No Person except a natural born Citizen, or a Citizen of the United States, at the time of the Adoption of this Constitution, shall be eligible to the Office of President; neither shall any Person be eligible to that Office who shall not have attained to the Age of thirty five Years, and been fourteen Years a Resident within the United States.

In Case of the Removal of the President from Office, or of his Death, Resignation, or Inability to discharge the Powers and Duties of the said Office, the Same shall devolve on the Vice President, and the Congress may by Law provide for the Case of Removal, Death, Resignation or Inability, both of the President and Vice President, declaring what Officer shall then act as President, and such Officer shall act accordingly, until the Disability be removed, or a President shall be elected.

The President shall, at stated Times, receive for his Services, a Compensation, which shall neither be encreased nor diminished during the Period for which he shall have been elected, and he shall not receive within that Period any other Emolument from the United States, or any of them.

Before he enters on the Execution of his Office, he shall take the following Oath or Affirmation:—"I do solemnly swear (or affirm) that I will faithfully execute the Office of President of the United States, and will to the best of my Ability, preserve, protect and defend the Constitution of the United States."

Section. 2.

The President shall be Commander in Chief of the Army and Navy of the United States, and of the Militia of the several States, when called into the actual Service of the United States; he may require the Opinion, in writing, of the principal Officer in each of the executive Departments, upon any Subject relating to the Duties of their respective Offices, and he shall have Power to grant Reprieves and Pardons for Offences against the United States, except in Cases of Impeachment.

He shall have Power, by and with the Advice and Consent of the Senate, to make Treaties, provided two thirds of the Senators present concur; and he shall nominate, and by and with the Advice and Consent of the Senate, shall appoint Ambassadors, other public Ministers and Consuls, Judges of the supreme Court, and all other Officers of the United States, whose Appointments are not herein otherwise provided for, and which shall be established by Law: but the Congress may by Law vest the Appointment of such inferior Officers, as they think proper, in the President alone, in the Courts of Law, or in the Heads of Departments.

The President shall have Power to fill up all Vacancies that may happen during the Recess of the Senate, by granting Commissions which shall expire at the End of their next Session.

Section. 3.

He shall from time to time give to the Congress Information of the State of the Union, and recommend to their Consideration such Measures as he shall judge necessary and expedient; he may, on extraordinary Occasions, convene both Houses, or either of them, and in Case of Disagreement between them, with Respect to the Time of Adjournment, he may adjourn them to such Time as he shall think proper; he shall receive Ambassadors and other public Ministers; he shall take Care that the Laws be faithfully executed, and shall Commission all the Officers of the United States.

Section. 4.

The President, Vice President and all civil Officers of the United States, shall be removed from Office on Impeachment for, and Conviction of, Treason, Bribery, or other high Crimes and Misdemeanors.

Article III

Section. 1.

The judicial Power of the United States, shall be vested in one supreme Court, and in such inferior Courts as the Congress may from time to time ordain and establish. The Judges, both of the supreme and inferior Courts, shall hold their Offices during good Behaviour, and shall, at stated Times, receive for their Services, a Compensation, which shall not be diminished during their Continuance in Office.

Section. 2.

The judicial Power shall extend to all Cases, in Law and Equity, arising under this Constitution, the Laws of the United States, and Treaties made, or which shall be made, under their Authority;—to all Cases affecting Ambassadors, other public Ministers and Consuls;—to all Cases of admiralty and maritime Jurisdiction;—to Controversies to which the United States shall be a Party;—to Controversies between two or more States;—between a State and Citizens of another State,—between Citizens of different States,—between Citizens of the same State claiming Lands under Grants of different States, and between a State, or the Citizens thereof, and foreign States, Citizens or Subjects.

In all Cases affecting Ambassadors, other public Ministers and Consuls, and those in which a State shall be Party, the supreme Court shall have original Jurisdiction. In all the other Cases before mentioned, the supreme Court shall have appellate Jurisdiction, both as to Law and Fact, with such Exceptions, and under such Regulations as the Congress shall make.

The Trial of all Crimes, except in Cases of Impeachment, shall be by Jury; and such Trial shall be held in the State where the said Crimes shall have been committed; but when not committed within any State, the Trial shall be at such Place or Places as the Congress may by Law have directed.

Section. 3.

Treason against the United States, shall consist only in levying War against them, or in adhering to their Enemies, giving them Aid and Comfort. No Person shall be convicted of Treason unless on the Testimony of two Witnesses to the same overt Act, or on Confession in open Court.

The Congress shall have Power to declare the Punishment of Treason, but no Attainder of Treason shall work Corruption of Blood, or Forfeiture except during the Life of the Person attainted.

Article. IV

Section. 1.

Full Faith and Credit shall be given in each State to the public Acts, Records, and judicial Proceedings of every other State. And the Congress may by general Laws prescribe the Manner in which such Acts, Records and Proceedings shall be proved, and the Effect thereof.

Section. 2.

The Citizens of each State shall be entitled to all Privileges and Immunities of Citizens in the several States.

A Person charged in any State with Treason, Felony, or other Crime, who shall flee from Justice, and be found in another State, shall on Demand of the executive Authority of the State from which he fled, be delivered up, to be removed to the State having Jurisdiction of the Crime.

No Person held to Service or Labour in one State, under the Laws thereof, escaping into another, shall, in Consequence of any Law or Regulation therein, be discharged from such Service or Labour, but shall be delivered up on Claim of the Party to whom such Service or Labour may be due.

Section. 3.

New States may be admitted by the Congress into this Union; but no new State shall be formed or erected within the Jurisdiction of any other State; nor any State be formed by the Junction of two or more States, or Parts of States, without the Consent of the Legislatures of the States concerned as well as of the Congress.

The Congress shall have Power to dispose of and make all needful Rules and Regulations respecting the Territory or other Property belonging to the United States; and nothing in this Constitution shall be so construed as to Prejudice any Claims of the United States, or of any particular State.

Section. 4.

The United States shall guarantee to every State in this Union a Republican Form of Government, and shall protect each of them against Invasion; and on Application of the Legislature, or of the Executive (when the Legislature cannot be convened), against domestic Violence.

Article. V

The Congress, whenever two thirds of both Houses shall deem it necessary, shall propose Amendments to this Constitution, or, on the Application of the Legislatures of two thirds of the several States, shall call a Convention for proposing Amendments, which, in either Case, shall be valid to all Intents and Purposes, as Part of this Constitution, when ratified by the Legislatures of three fourths of the several States, or by Conventions in three fourths thereof, as the one or the other Mode of Ratification may be proposed by the Congress; Provided that no Amendment which may be made prior to the Year One thousand eight hundred and eight shall in any Manner affect the first and fourth Clauses in the Ninth Section of the first Article; and that no State, without its Consent, shall be deprived of its equal Suffrage in the Senate.

Article. VI

All Debts contracted and Engagements entered into, before the Adoption of this Constitution, shall be as valid against the United States under this Constitution, as under the Confederation.

This Constitution, and the Laws of the United States which shall be made in Pursuance thereof; and all Treaties made, or which shall be made, under the Authority of the United States, shall be the supreme Law of the Land; and the Judges in every State shall be bound thereby, any Thing in the Constitution or Laws of any State to the Contrary notwithstanding.

The Senators and Representatives before mentioned, and the Members of the several State Legislatures, and all executive and judicial Officers, both of the United States and of the several States, shall be bound by Oath or Affirmation, to support this Constitution; but no religious Test shall ever be required as a Qualification to any Office or public Trust under the United States.

Article. VII

The Ratification of the Conventions of nine States, shall be sufficient for the Establishment of this Constitution between the States so ratifying the Same.

The Word, "the," being interlined between the seventh and eighth Lines of the first Page, The Word "Thirty" being partly written on an Erazure in the fifteenth Line of the first Page, The Words "is tried" being interlined between the thirty second and thirty third Lines of the first Page and the Word "the" being interlined between the forty third and forty fourth Lines of the second Page.

Attest William Jackson Secretary, done in Convention by the Unanimous Consent of the States present the Seventeenth Day of September in the Year of our Lord one thousand seven hundred and Eighty seven and of the Independance of the United States of America the Twelfth In witness whereof We have hereunto subscribed our Names, G°. Washington, *Presidt and deputy from Virginia*

Delaware
Geo: Read
Gunning Bedford jun
John Dickinson
Richard Bassett
Jaco: Broom

Maryland
James McHenry
Dan of St Thos.
Jenifer
Danl. Carroll

Virginia
John Blair
James Madison Jr.

North Carolina
Wm. Blount
Richd. Dobbs
Spaight
Hu Williamson

South Carolina
J. Rutledge
Charles Cotesworth
Pinckney
Charles Pinckney
Pierce Butler

Georgia
William Few
Abr Baldwin

New Hampshire
John Langdon
Nicholas Gilman

Massachusetts
Nathaniel Gorham
Rufus King

Connecticut
Wm. Saml. Johnson
Roger Sherman

New York
Alexander Hamilton

New Jersey
Wil: Livingston
David Brearley
Wm. Paterson
Jona: Dayton

Pensylvania
B Franklin
Thomas Mifflin
Robt. Morris
Geo. Clymer
Thos. FitzSimons
Jared Ingersoll
James Wilson
Gouv Morris

Enactment of the Bill of Rights of the United States of America (1791)

The first ten Amendments to the Constitution make up the Bill of Rights. Written by James Madison in response to calls from several states for greater constitutional protection for individual liberties, the Bill of Rights lists specific prohibitions on governmental power. The Virginia Declaration of Rights, written by George Mason, strongly influenced Madison.

One of the contention points between Federalists and Anti-Federalists was the Constitution's lack of a bill of rights that would place specific limits on government power.

Federalists argued that the Constitution did not need a bill of rights because the people and the states kept powers not explicitly given to the federal government.

Anti-Federalists held that a *bill of rights* was necessary to safeguard individual liberty.

Madison, then a member of the U.S. House of Representatives, went through the Constitution itself, making changes where he thought most appropriate.

Several Representatives, led by Roger Sherman, objected that Congress had no authority to change the wording of the Constitution. Therefore, Madison's changes were presented as a list of amendments that would follow Article VII.

The House approved 17 amendments. Of these 17, the Senate approved 12. Those 12 were sent to the states for approval in August of 1789. Of those 12 proposed amendments, 10 were quickly ratified. Virginia's legislature became the last to ratify the Amendments on December 15, 1791. These Amendments are the Bill of Rights.

The Bill of Rights is a list of limits on government power. For example, what the Founders saw as the natural right of individuals to speak and worship freely was protected by the First Amendment's prohibitions on Congress from making laws establishing a religion or abridging freedom of speech.

Another example is the natural right to be free from the government's unreasonable intrusion in one's home was safeguarded by the Fourth Amendment's warrant requirements.

Other precursors to the Bill of Rights include English documents such as the Magna Carta[1], the Petition of Rights, the English Bill of Rights, and the Massachusetts Body of Liberties.

The Magna Carta illustrates Compact Theory[1] as well as initial strides toward limited government. Its provisions address individual rights and political rights. Latin for "Great Charter," the Magna Carta was written by Barons in Runnymede, England, and forced on the King.

Although the protections were generally limited to the prerogatives of the Barons, the Magna Carta embodied the general principle that the King accepted limitations on his rule. These included the fundamental acknowledgment that the king was not above the law.

Included in the Magna Carta are protections for the English church, petitioning the king, freedom from the forced quarter of troops and unreasonable searches, due process and fair trial

---

137

protections, and freedom from excessive fines. These protections can be found in the First, Third, Fourth, Fifth, Sixth, and Eighth Amendments to the Constitution.

The Magna Carta is the oldest compact in England. The Mayflower Compact, the Fundamental Orders of Connecticut, and the Albany Plan are examples from the American colonies.

The Articles of Confederation was a compact among the states, and the Constitution creates a compact based on a federal system between the national government, state governments, and the people. The Hayne-Webster Debate focused on the compact created by the Constitution.

---

[1] Philosophers including Thomas Hobbes, John Locke, and Jean-Jacques Rousseau theorized that peoples' condition in a "state of nature" (that is, outside of society) is one of freedom, but that freedom inevitably degrades into war, chaos, or debilitating competition without the benefit of a system of laws and government. They reasoned, therefore, that for their happiness, individuals willingly trade some of their natural freedom in exchange for the protections provided by the government.

The Bill of Rights: Amendments I–X

Amendment I

Congress shall make no law respecting an establishment of religion, or prohibiting the free exercise thereof; or abridging the freedom of speech, or of the press; or the right of the people peaceably to assemble, and to petition the government for a redress of grievances.

Amendment II

A well regulated militia, being necessary to the security of a free state, the right of the people to keep and bear arms, shall not be infringed.

Amendment III

No soldier shall, in time of peace be quartered in any house, without the consent of the owner, nor in time of war, but in a manner to be prescribed by law.

Amendment IV

The right of the people to be secure in their persons, houses, papers, and effects, against unreasonable searches and seizures, shall not be violated, and no warrants shall issue, but upon probable cause, supported by oath or affirmation, and particularly describing the place to be searched, and the persons or things to be seized.

Amendment V

No person shall be held to answer for a capital, or otherwise infamous crime, unless on a presentment or indictment of a grand jury, except in cases arising in the land or naval forces, or in the militia, when in actual service in time of war or public danger; nor shall any person be subject for the same offense to be twice put in jeopardy of life or limb; nor shall be compelled in any criminal case to be a witness against himself, nor be deprived of life, liberty, or property, without due process of law; nor shall private property be taken for public use, without just compensation.

Amendment VI

In all criminal prosecutions, the accused shall enjoy the right to a speedy and public trial, by an impartial jury of the state and district wherein the crime shall have been committed, which district shall have been previously ascertained by law, and to be informed of the nature and cause of the accusation; to be confronted with the witnesses against him; to have compulsory process for obtaining witnesses in his favor, and to have the assistance of counsel for his defense.

Amendment VII

In suits at common law, where the value in controversy shall exceed twenty dollars, the right of trial by jury shall be preserved, and no fact tried by a jury, shall be otherwise reexamined in any court of the United States, than according to the rules of the common law.

Amendment VIII

Excessive bail shall not be required, nor excessive fines imposed, nor cruel and unusual punishments inflicted.

Amendment IX

The enumeration in the Constitution, of certain rights, shall not be construed to deny or disparage others retained by the people.

Amendment X

The powers not delegated to the United States by the Constitution, nor prohibited by it to the states, are reserved to the states respectively, or to the people.

Constitutional Amendments XI–XXVII

AMENDMENT XI

Passed by Congress March 4, 1794. Ratified February 7, 1795.

Note: Article III, section 2, of the Constitution was modified by amendment 11.

The Judicial power of the United States shall not be construed to extend to any suit in law or equity, commenced or prosecuted against one of the United States by Citizens of another State, or by Citizens or Subjects of any Foreign State.

AMENDMENT XII

Passed by Congress December 9, 1803. Ratified June 15, 1804.

Note: A portion of Article II, section 1 of the Constitution was superseded by the 12th amendment.

The Electors shall meet in their respective states and vote by ballot for President and Vice-President, one of whom, at least, shall not be an inhabitant of the same state with themselves; they shall name in their ballots the person voted for as President, and in distinct ballots the person voted for as Vice-President, and they shall make distinct lists of all persons voted for as President, and of all persons voted for as Vice-President, and of the number of votes for each, which lists they shall sign and certify, and transmit sealed to the seat of the government of the United States, directed to the President of the Senate; -- the President of the Senate shall, in the presence of the Senate and House of Representatives, open all the certificates and the votes shall then be counted; -- The person having the greatest number of votes for President, shall be the President, if such number be a majority of the whole number of Electors appointed; and if no person have such majority, then from the persons having the highest numbers not exceeding three on the list of those voted for as President, the House of Representatives shall choose immediately, by ballot, the President. But in choosing the President, the votes shall be taken by states, the representation from each state having one vote; a quorum for this purpose shall consist of a member or members from two-thirds of the states, and a majority of all the states shall be necessary to a choice. [And if the House of Representatives shall not choose a President whenever the right of choice shall devolve upon them, before the fourth day of March next following, then the Vice-President shall act as President, as in case of the death or other constitutional disability of the President. --]* The person having the greatest number of votes as Vice-President, shall be the Vice-President, if such number be a majority of the whole number of Electors appointed, and if no person have a majority, then from the two highest numbers on the list, the Senate shall choose the Vice-President; a quorum for the purpose shall consist of two-thirds of the whole number of Senators, and a majority of the whole number shall be necessary to a choice. But no person constitutionally ineligible to the office of President shall be eligible to that of Vice-President of the United States.

Superseded by section 3 of the 20th Amendment.

AMENDMENT XIII

Passed by Congress January 31, 1865. Ratified December 6, 1865.

Note: A portion of Article IV, section 2, of the Constitution was superseded by the 13th amendment.

Section 1.

Neither slavery nor involuntary servitude, except as a punishment for crime whereof the party shall have been duly convicted, shall exist within the United States, or any place subject to their jurisdiction.

Section 2.

Congress shall have power to enforce this article by appropriate legislation.

AMENDMENT XIV

Passed by Congress June 13, 1866. Ratified July 9, 1868.

Note: Article I, section 2, of the Constitution was modified by section 2 of the 14th amendment.

Section 1.

All persons born or naturalized in the United States, and subject to the jurisdiction thereof, are citizens of the United States and of the State wherein they reside. No State shall make or enforce any law which shall abridge the privileges or immunities of citizens of the United States; nor shall any State deprive any person of life, liberty, or property, without due process of law; nor deny to any person within its jurisdiction the equal protection of the laws.

Section 2.

Representatives shall be apportioned among the several States according to their respective numbers, counting the whole number of persons in each State, excluding Indians not taxed. But when the right to vote at any election for the choice of electors for President and Vice-President of the United States, Representatives in Congress, the Executive and Judicial officers of a State, or the members of the Legislature thereof, is denied to any of the male inhabitants of such State, being twenty-one years of age,* and citizens of the United States, or in any way abridged, except for participation in rebellion, or other crime, the basis of representation therein shall be reduced in the proportion which the number of such male citizens shall bear to the whole number of male citizens twenty-one years of age in such State.

Section 3.

No person shall be a Senator or Representative in Congress, or elector of President and Vice-President, or hold any office, civil or military, under the United States, or under any State, who, having previously taken an oath, as a member of Congress, or as an officer of the United States, or as a member of any State legislature, or as an executive or judicial officer of any State, to support the Constitution of the United States, shall have engaged in insurrection or rebellion against the same, or given aid or comfort to the enemies thereof. But Congress may by a vote of two-thirds of each House, remove such disability.

Section 4.

The validity of the public debt of the United States, authorized by law, including debts incurred for payment of pensions and bounties for services in suppressing insurrection or rebellion, shall not be questioned. But neither the United States nor any State shall assume or pay any debt or obligation incurred in aid of insurrection or rebellion against the United States, or any claim for the loss or emancipation of any slave; but all such debts, obligations and claims shall be held illegal and void.

Section 5.

The Congress shall have the power to enforce, by appropriate legislation, the provisions of this article.

*Changed by section 1 of the 26th Amendment.

AMENDMENT XV

Passed by Congress February 26, 1869. Ratified February 3, 1870.

Section 1.

The right of citizens of the United States to vote shall not be denied or abridged by the United States or by any State on account of race, color, or previous condition of servitude.

Section 2.

The Congress shall have the power to enforce this article by appropriate legislation.

AMENDMENT XVI

Passed by Congress July 2, 1909. Ratified February 3, 1913.

Note: Article I, section 9, of the Constitution was modified by amendment 16.

The Congress shall have power to lay and collect taxes on incomes, from whatever source derived, without apportionment among the several States, and without regard to any census or enumeration.

AMENDMENT XVII

Passed by Congress May 13, 1912. Ratified April 8, 1913.

Note: Article I, section 3, of the Constitution was modified by the 17th Amendment.

The Senate of the United States shall be composed of two Senators from each State, elected by the people thereof, for six years; and each Senator shall have one vote. The electors in each State shall have the qualifications requisite for electors of the most numerous branch of the State legislatures.

When vacancies happen in the representation of any State in the Senate, the executive authority of such State shall issue writs of election to fill such vacancies: *Provided*, That the legislature of any State may empower the executive thereof to make temporary appointments until the people fill the vacancies by election as the legislature may direct.

This amendment shall not be so construed as to affect the election or term of any Senator chosen before it becomes valid as part of the Constitution.

AMENDMENT XVIII

Passed by Congress December 18, 1917. Ratified January 16, 1919. Repealed by Amendment 21.

Section 1.

After one year from the ratification of this article the manufacture, sale, or transportation of intoxicating liquors within, the importation thereof into, or the exportation thereof from the United States and all territory subject to the jurisdiction thereof for beverage purposes is hereby prohibited.

Section 2.

The Congress and the several States shall have concurrent power to enforce this article by appropriate legislation.

Section 3.

This article shall be inoperative unless it shall have been ratified as an amendment to the Constitution by the legislatures of the several States, as provided in the Constitution, within seven years from the date of the submission hereof to the States by the Congress.

AMENDMENT XIX

Passed by Congress June 4, 1919. Ratified August 18, 1920.

The right of citizens of the United States to vote shall not be denied or abridged by the United States or by any State on account of sex.

Congress shall have power to enforce this article by appropriate legislation.

AMENDMENT XX

Passed by Congress March 2, 1932. Ratified January 23, 1933.

Note: Article I, section 4, of the Constitution was modified by section 2 of this Amendment. In addition, a portion of the 12th Amendment was superseded by section 3.

Section 1.

The terms of the President and the Vice President shall end at noon on the 20th day of January, and the terms of Senators and Representatives at noon on the 3d day of January, of the years in which such terms would have ended if this article had not been ratified; and the terms of their successors shall then begin.

Section 2.

The Congress shall assemble at least once in every year, and such meeting shall begin at noon on the 3d day of January, unless they shall by law appoint a different day.

Section 3.

If, at the time fixed for the beginning of the term of the President, the President elect shall have died, the Vice President elect shall become President. If a President shall not have been chosen before the time fixed for the beginning of his term, or if the President elect shall have failed to qualify, then the Vice President elect shall act as President until a President shall have qualified; and the Congress may by law provide for the case wherein neither a President elect nor a Vice President elect shall have qualified, declaring who shall then act as President, or the manner in which one who is to act shall be selected, and such person shall act accordingly until a President or Vice President shall have qualified.

Section 4.

The Congress may by law provide for the case of the death of any of the persons from whom the House of Representatives may choose a President whenever the right of choice shall have devolved upon them, and for the case of the death of any of the persons from whom the Senate may choose a Vice President whenever the right of choice shall have devolved upon them.

Section 5.

Sections 1 and 2 shall take effect on the 15th day of October following the ratification of this article.

Section 6.

This article shall be inoperative unless it shall have been ratified as an amendment to the Constitution by the legislatures of three-fourths of the several States within seven years from the date of its submission.

AMENDMENT XXI

Passed by Congress February 20, 1933. Ratified December 5, 1933.

Section 1.

The eighteenth article of amendment to the Constitution of the United States is hereby repealed.

Section 2.

The transportation or importation into any State, Territory, or possession of the United States for delivery or use therein of intoxicating liquors, in violation of the laws thereof, is hereby prohibited.

Section 3.

This article shall be inoperative unless it shall have been ratified as an amendment to the Constitution by conventions in the several States, as provided in the Constitution, within seven years from the date of the submission hereof to the States by the Congress.

AMENDMENT XXII

Passed by Congress March 21, 1947. Ratified February 27, 1951.

Section 1.

No person shall be elected to the office of the President more than twice, and no person who has held the office of President, or acted as President, for more than two years of a term to which some other person was elected President shall be elected to the office of the President more than once. But this Article shall not apply to any person holding the office of President when this Article was proposed by the Congress, and shall not prevent any person who may be holding the office of President, or acting as President, during the term within which this Article becomes operative from holding the office of President or acting as President during the remainder of such term.

Section 2.

This article shall be inoperative unless it shall have been ratified as an amendment to the Constitution by the legislatures of three-fourths of the several States within seven years from the date of its submission to the States by the Congress.

AMENDMENT XXIII

Passed by Congress June 16, 1960. Ratified March 29, 1961.

Section 1.

The District constituting the seat of Government of the United States shall appoint in such manner as the Congress may direct:

A number of electors of President and Vice President equal to the whole number of Senators and Representatives in Congress to which the District would be entitled if it were a State, but in no event more than the least populous State; they shall be in addition to those appointed by the States, but they shall be considered, for the purposes of the election of President and Vice President, to be electors appointed by a State; and they shall meet in the District and perform such duties as provided by the twelfth article of amendment.

Section 2.

The Congress shall have power to enforce this article by appropriate legislation.

AMENDMENT XXIV

Passed by Congress August 27, 1962. Ratified January 23, 1964.

Section 1.

The right of citizens of the United States to vote in any primary or other election for President or Vice President, for electors for President or Vice President, or for Senator or Representative in Congress, shall not be denied or abridged by the United States or any State by reason of failure to pay any poll tax or other tax.

Section 2.

The Congress shall have power to enforce this article by appropriate legislation.

AMENDMENT XXV

Passed by Congress July 6, 1965. Ratified February 10, 1967.

Note: Article II, section 1, of the Constitution was affected by the 25th amendment.

Section 1.

In case of the removal of the President from office or of his death or resignation, the Vice President shall become President.

Section 2.

Whenever there is a vacancy in the office of the Vice President, the President shall nominate a Vice President who shall take office upon confirmation by a majority vote of both Houses of Congress.

Section 3.

Whenever the President transmits to the President pro tempore of the Senate and the Speaker of the House of Representatives his written declaration that he is unable to discharge the powers and duties of his office, and until he transmits to them a written declaration to the contrary, such powers and duties shall be discharged by the Vice President as Acting President.

Section 4.

Whenever the Vice President and a majority of either the principal officers of the executive departments or of such other body as Congress may by law provide, transmit to the President pro tempore of the Senate and the Speaker of the House of Representatives their written declaration that the President is unable to discharge the powers and duties of his office, the Vice President shall immediately assume the powers and duties of the office as Acting President.

Thereafter, when the President transmits to the President pro tempore of the Senate and the Speaker of the House of Representatives his written declaration that no inability exists, he shall resume the powers and duties of his office unless the Vice President and a majority of either the principal officers of the executive department or of such other body as Congress may by law provide, transmit within four days to the President pro tempore of the Senate and the Speaker of the House of Representatives their written declaration that the President is unable to discharge the powers and duties of his office. Thereupon Congress shall decide the issue, assembling within forty-eight hours for that purpose if not in session. If the Congress, within twenty-one days after receipt of the latter written declaration, or, if Congress is not in session, within twenty-one days after Congress is required to assemble, determines by two-thirds vote of both Houses that the President is unable to discharge the powers and duties of his office, the Vice President shall continue to discharge the same as Acting President; otherwise, the President shall resume the powers and duties of his office.

AMENDMENT XXVI

Passed by Congress March 23, 1971. Ratified July 1, 1971.

Note: Amendment 14, section 2, of the Constitution was modified by section 1 of the 26th amendment.

Section 1.
The right of citizens of the United States, who are eighteen years of age or older, to vote shall not be denied or abridged by the United States or by any State on account of age.

Section 2.
The Congress shall have power to enforce this article by appropriate legislation.

AMENDMENT XXVII

Originally proposed Sept. 25, 1789. Ratified May 7, 1992.

No law, varying the compensation for the services of the Senators and Representatives, shall take effect, until an election of Representatives shall have intervened

States' Rights Under the U.S. Constitution

Selective incorporation under the 14th Amendment

The U.S. Constitution has Articles and Amendments that established constitutional rights.

The provisions in the Bill of Rights (i.e., the first ten Amendments to the Constitution) were initially binding upon only the federal government.

In time, most of these provisions became binding upon the states through *selective incorporation* into the *due process clause* of the 14th Amendment (i.e., reverse incorporation).

When a provision is made binding on a state, a state can no longer restrict the rights guaranteed in that provision.

The 1st Amendment guarantees the freedoms of speech, press, religion, and assembly.

The 5th Amendment protects the right to grand jury proceedings in federal criminal cases.

The 6th Amendment guarantees a right to confront witnesses (i.e., Confrontation Clause).

The right to confront witnesses was not *selectively incorporated* into the due process clause of the 14th Amendment and is not binding upon the states.

Therefore, persons involved in state criminal proceedings as a defendant have no federal constitutional right to grand jury proceedings.

Whether an individual has a right to a grand jury becomes a question of state law.

The 10th Amendment, which is part of the Bill of Rights, was ratified on December 15, 1791. It states the Constitution's principle of federalism by providing that powers not granted to the federal government by the Constitution, nor prohibited to the States, are reserved to the States or the people.

Federalism in the United States

Federalism in the United States is the evolving relationship between state governments and the federal government.

The American government has evolved from a system of dual federalism to associative federalism.

In "Federalist No. 46," James Madison wrote that the states and national government "are in fact but different agents and trustees of the people, constituted with different powers."

Alexander Hamilton, in "Federalist No. 28," suggested that both levels of government would exercise authority to the citizens' benefit: "If their [the peoples'] rights are invaded by either, they can make use of the other as the instrument of redress."[3]

Because the states were preexisting political entities, the U.S. Constitution did not need to define or explain federalism in one section, but it often mentions the rights and responsibilities of state governments and state officials in relation to the federal government.

The federal government has certain *express powers* (also called *enumerated powers*), which are powers spelled out in the Constitution, including the right to levy taxes, declare war, and regulate interstate and foreign commerce.

Also, the *Necessary and Proper Clause* gives the federal government the *implied power* to pass any law "necessary and proper" to execute its express powers.

Enumerated powers of the Federal Government are contained in Article I, Section 8 of the U.S. Constitution.

Other powers—the *reserved powers*—are reserved to the people or the states under the 10th Amendment. The Supreme Court decision significantly expanded the power delegated to the federal government in *McCulloch v. Maryland* (1819) and the 13th, 14th and 15th, Amendments to the Constitution following the Civil War.

Law Essentials series

Constitutional Law	Criminal Law and Criminal Procedure
Contracts	Business Associations
Evidence	Conflict of Laws
Real Property	Family Law
Torts	Secured Transactions
Civil Procedure	Trusts and Estates

Visit our Amazon store

Comprehensive Glossary of Legal Terms

Over 2,100 essential legal terms defined and explained. An excellent reference source for law students, practitioners and readers seeking an understanding of legal vocabulary and its application.

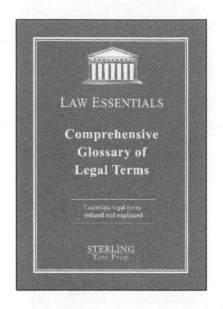

Landmark U.S. Supreme Court Cases: Essential Summaries

Learn important constitutional cases that shaped American law. Understand how the evolving needs of society intersect with the U.S. Constitution. Short summaries of seminal Supreme Court cases focused on issues and holdings.

Visit our Amazon store

Frank J. Addivinola, Ph.D., J.D., L.LM., MBA

The lead author and chief editor of this preparation guide is Dr. Frank Addivinola. With his outstanding education, professional training, legal and business experience, and university teaching, Dr. Addivinola lent his expertise to develop this book.

Attorney Frank Addivinola is admitted to practice law in several jurisdictions. He has served as an academic advisor and mentor for students and practitioners.

Dr. Addivinola holds an undergraduate degree from Williams College. He completed his Masters at Harvard University, Masters in Biotechnology at Johns Hopkins University, Masters in Technology Management and MBA at the University of Maryland University College, J.D. and L.LM. from Suffolk University, and Ph.D. in Law and Public Policy from Northeastern University.

During his extensive teaching career, Dr. Addivinola taught university courses in Introduction to Law and developed law coursebooks. He received several awards for community service, research, and presentations.

Made in the USA
Monee, IL
03 October 2021